Roots of Caring,
Sharing, and Helping

A Series of Books in Psychology

Editors:
Richard C. Atkinson
Jonathan Freedman
Gardner Lindzey
Richard F. Thompson

Roots of Caring, Sharing, and Helping

THE DEVELOPMENT OF PROSOCIAL BEHAVIOR IN CHILDREN

PAUL MUSSEN

UNIVERSITY OF CALIFORNIA, BERKELEY

NANCY EISENBERG-BERG

ARIZONA STATE UNIVERSITY

W. H. FREEMAN AND COMPANY
San Francisco

Library of Congress Cataloging in Publication Data

Mussen, Paul Henry.
  Roots of caring, sharing, and helping.

  (A series of books in psychology)
  Bibliography: p.
  Includes index.
    1. Socialization. 2. Child development.
I. Eisenberg-Berg, Nancy. II. Title.
HQ783.M83   301.15'72   77–22750
ISBN 0–7167–0045–X
ISBN 0–7167–0044–1 pbk.

Printed in the United States of America

9 8 7 6 5 4 3 2 1

Contents

Preface

Among the many self-evident requirements of modern society, the needs for improved moral quality and for increased concern with the welfare of others are prominent. To deal with these needs—or at least to halt what seems to be progressive deterioration in morality—requires scientific information about how moral precepts and humane behavior are acquired, develop, and become modified. This kind of knowledge would undoubtedly be of great practical value in training children to be more prosocial—that is, more kind, considerate, and altruistic—in their relations with others. The principles of prosocial development, if fully understood, might also be applicable in the modification of adult social behavior.

Despite long-standing and urgent needs for scientific understanding of moral issues, systematic investigation of moral development is a relatively recent phenomenon. In the last ten or fifteen years, there has been a dramatic increase in research activity in this aspect of social development. By now, a large but somewhat diffuse body of information has been accumulated and published. The field (or subfield) of moral development—cognitive and behavioral—is flourishing, and the outlook for significant theoretical and pragmatic contributions in the future is very promising.

For these reasons, this is an appropriate time to take stock of the present state of the field, to evaluate its accomplishments and deficiencies, and to delineate major gaps in our knowledge and theoretical understanding. Our goals in writing this book included summarizing the available information in a coherent way, examining findings on the major determinants of prosocial behavior, assessing methods of study, and, wherever possible, integrating fundamental theories and conceptualizations with research data. But we hoped to provide more than an organized survey of the available literature. Throughout our review, we attempted to highlight the broader, applied implications of theory and research findings, while specifying research needs, weighing alternative research strategies, and suggesting fruitful and exciting issues for future investigation. Perhaps immodestly, we hoped to help give shape and direction to an emerging field (or subfield) that, in our view, has enormous potential.

Our survey is admittedly not exhaustive, but we believe we have included *examples* of every *major type* of research on the development of prosocial behavior. Given the constraints of a short book, we could not describe or summarize every important study we reviewed. Some research work that yielded relevant information is not included.

A number of reviews of research, referenced in the Notes section, have been most helpful in preparing this book. We acknowledge our indebtedness to the authors of these reviews, James Bryant, Martin Hoffman, Dennis Krebs, J. Philippe Rushton, Ervin Staub, and Derek Wright, and we benefited greatly from reading parts of William Damon's forthcoming book, *The Social World of the Child.*

We also wish to express our special gratitude to J. Philippe Rushton of the University of Toronto, who read the entire manuscript and made many valuable suggestions, and to Vivien March, who helped enormously in preparing the manuscript.

Paul Mussen
Nancy Eisenberg-Berg

June 1977
Berkeley, California

Roots of Caring,
Sharing, and Helping

Introduction

What is fundamental in human nature and behavior? What traits and values are inherent in humanity itself? Reflecting on these questions, we might reasonably conclude that propensities for positive social action—for sympathy, generosity, and cooperation—are far less powerful than dispositions toward destruction and inhumanity. The mass media horrify us daily with news of immense cruelties and senseless killings but seldom lift our spirits with accounts of ennobling deeds of kindness, altruism, or self-sacrifice. Contemporary horrors (wartime atrocities, civil wars, racial conflicts, terrorists capturing hostages, mushrooming rates of rape and other violent crimes) seem to be only extreme expressions of a deplorable but prevalent human condition. In complex societies such as our own there is a wide spectrum of individual differences or variations in practically all personal attributes and styles of social interactions. In our daily lives, in our homes and communities, at work and at school, we encounter all degrees and varieties of egotism and self-seeking behaviors as well as kind and sympathetic actions. Some of the people we deal with seem to be of uncompromising selfishness, pursuing their own interests and goals relentlessly without regard to the interests of others. Fortunately, others have predominant orientations of an opposite sort; their overriding concerns are with the "social good" and welfare of others. Of course, most people stand somewhere between these two extremes on a continuum from unmitigated selfishness to total concern with others.

The norms or standards of social orientations and consideration of others vary from culture to culture and from society to society. Consider the Ik, the mountain people of Uganda, described by the anthropologist Colin Turnbull.[1] This small tribe of hunters once had an established social structure and culture, with laws, mores, and customs, until political and technological changes deprived them of their hunting grounds. Then their social organization disintegrated and they broke into small ruthless bands concerned only with personal survival. They became dehumanized, savage; lying, stealing, plotting, scheming, deceit, treachery—even killing—became aspects of their "normal" way of life. No one seemed to have any compassion for anyone else, not even for mates, parents, or children. Caring for others, generosity, kindness (the kinds of behavior we label prosocial) simply did not seem to exist in this group. If this is an accurate representation of the "natural" or "basic" human condition, we should be pessimistic about the possibilities of improving the world.

We might be more optimistic if there were fewer people like the Ik, and more who followed the traditional Hopi way of life. In the view of this Arizona Indian tribe, all aspects of the universe, human and natural, are interrelated and interdependent. Consequently, community cooperation is regarded as essential for survival, and most, if not all, of what an individual thinks and does has reference to the group. From earliest childhood onward, nothing is more important to the Hopi than having a "Hopi good heart," defined as trust and respect for others; concern for everyone's rights, welfare, and feelings; inner peacefulness, and avoidance of conflict. In the Hopi family the needs of the individual and those of the household are all served through helpfulness and cooperation; family interactions are not controlled by rules and regulations. The ideals of personal character and the compelling motives of the Hopi include cooperativeness, industriousness, compliance, and an unaggressive approach to people and to situations. Not surprisingly, competition, dissension, and self-assertion are strikingly absent in the traditional Hopi community.[2]

Does the Hopi life style, rather than the Ik's, reflect the fundamental, deeply ingrained, and enduring components of human nature? Unfortunately, there is no reason to believe that this is the case. The age-old perplexing problem of "what is basic human nature" has never been resolved and perhaps it never will be. The individual's behavior, moral or immoral, admirable or deplorable, is the outcome of a complex and intricate network of interacting biological, social, psychological, economic, and historical events—the result of biological (genetic) potentialities interacting with environmental (learning) experiences.

The Definition of Prosocial Behavior

In their everyday existence, the Hopi engage in a great deal of prosocial behavior; the Ik display very little. Now that we have given some examples, we must define our terms explicitly. Prosocial behavior refers to actions that are intended to aid or benefit another person or group of people without the actor's anticipation of external rewards. Such actions often entail some cost, self-sacrifice, or risk on the part of the actor. A wide variety of behaviors is encompassed by this rubric, including generosity, altruism, sympathy, helping people in distress by giving material or psychological assistance, sharing possessions, donating to charity, and participating in activities designed to improve the general welfare by reducing social injustices, inequalities, and brutality. Actually, although theorists and investigators often make inferences about the motives that activate prosocial acts, these motivations have seldom been explored directly (see also pp. 163–164). Internalized motives and self-rewards (intrinsic rewards such as increased self-esteem or feelings of satisfaction, pleasure, or pride following an action) seem to determine many prosocial acts, although it may be difficult to identify or to demonstrate these motives empirically.[3] It seems likely that with increasing age, children's motives for assisting others become less dependent on external rewards, punishments, and approval of authority and, in this sense, more internalized.[4]

Norms and Behavior

The principal focus of this book is on prosocial *acts,* that is, on overt responses and manifest prosocial *behavior.* For this reason, from the outset we must draw attention to several important distinctions.

First, the *acquisition* (*learning*) of prosocial behavior must be clearly differentiated from its *performance.* An individual may have learned a particular prosocial response but may actually manifest it only on certain occasions or under certain circumstances. Consider this simple instance: a youngster has learned that he or she should come to the aid of another youngster who is being picked on unfairly. The youngster often does this. But under circumstances in which this response is potentially dangerous (for example, if the aggressors are big and tough and the would-be altruist risks becoming another victim) he or she may leave the scene rather than try to aid the victim.

Knowledge of societal norms may be quite separate from conduct that conforms to these norms. Some prevalent norms (cultural expectations or prescriptions for how one *ought* to behave) are learned early in life, probably by identification and imitation of the behavior of others. According to the *norm of reciprocity,* people should help those who have helped them; that is, a recipient of assistance should repay the benefactor.[5] The *norm of social responsibility* prescribes that we should assist others who depend on us and need help. When this norm is internalized, giving becomes an end in itself and we "act on behalf of others, not for material gain or social approval but for [our] own self-approval, for the self-administered rewards arising from doing what is 'right.'"[6] By the age of eight or nine, children have learned the norm of responsibility and express their agreement with it. They can explain the norm to other children and judge others' behavior on the basis of its conformity to this norm. Yet this knowledge of the norms per se does not ordinarily instigate prosocial actions; children's endorsement of the norm is not significantly related to generosity in donating to the needy.[7]

To act in accordance with learned or internalized norms, the child must first perceive the other person's needs, interpret them accurately, and recognize that he or she can be helped. In addition, the child must feel competent in this situation, that is, capable of providing what is needed, and the cost or risk entailed in helping must not be prohibitive. Unless these preconditions are met, even the child who knows the norm of

social responsibility is not likely to render aid. A self-con-
cerned or egocentric youngster may not be aware of the needs
of others or may be unable to interpret these needs accurately,
and many failures to conform with the norm of assisting others
are the results of ignorance of how to help in certain situations.
In short, while societal norms bearing on prosocial behavior
are undoubtedly widely accepted, even among children, they
guide behavior only some of the time and under particular
circumstances. Internalization of norms is not an adequate
explanation or predictor of prosocial behavior; in fact, there is
very little evidence that knowledge of norms exerts control of
children's actions.[8]

Prosocial *behavior* must also be clearly distinguished from
moral *judgment,* a term that refers to the *cognitive* aspects of
morality—conceptualizations and reasoning about moral issues. In recent years, much of the research in moral development, stimulated largely by the creative theories and
investigations of Jean Piaget and of Lawrence Kohlberg, has
been centered on moral judgment. As we shall see later, moral
judgment and moral conduct are associated, but there is
hardly a one-to-one correspondence between them. An individual may possess mature, sophisticated concepts and judgments about moral issues, but this does not necessarily imply
that he or she will ordinarily behave in prosocial ways.

It is important to make these distinctions at this point
because all the key variables on which we will concentrate
pertain to prosocial *actions.* Variables such as a knowledge of
societal norms, motives, moral conceptualizations, and moral
judgments are extremely important topics in their own right
and are the subjects of a great deal of important research and
theory.[9] But, in this book, we are concerned with them only as
they relate to prosocial conduct.

The Purpose of This Book

Although it may be assumed that all human beings have the *potential* for acquiring prosocial behavior, even in substantial amounts, the behavior itself—the forms and frequency of prosocial actions—must be *learned*. For example, if a young Ik infant were adopted by Hopis and reared in the foster parents' culture, he or she would act as a Hopi, not as an Ik. And a Hopi raised from early childhood among the Ik would show Ik rather than Hopi characteristics.

This book is designed to provide an analytical examination of what is known about how prosocial behavior develops, and the processes or mechanisms underlying that development. How are children socialized to behave in prosocial ways? What personal attributes or capabilities, what environmental conditions facilitate or inhibit expressions of generosity, helping, and altruism? These are some of the primary issues explored in this volume.

Intimately related to these questions are questions pertaining to *variability* in prosocial behavior. Two kinds of variability are of concern: differences among individuals and variations in an individual's behavior from time to time. Why do some people possess strong predispositions toward prosocial conduct, while others show very little concern about others? What are the *antecedents* of high levels of altruism and sharing?

Attempting to understand the first kind of variance (variance among people or individual differences) inevitably brings us to a scrutiny of critical questions of socialization and children's interactions with, and reactions to, the major agents of socialization: parents, teachers, peers, cultural and religious institutions, the mass media. How do the values of the culture affect the child's tendencies to help others? What kinds of

child-rearing practices or parental attitudes foster or inhibit
the development of prosocial behavior? What role, if any, do
peers play in shaping the degree and intensity of the child's
predispositions to generosity or altruism? Do school and the
mass media have significant impacts? We shall examine what
is known about how each of these agents affects the strength
of the individual's prosocial tendencies. The key to understanding individual differences in prosocial behavior lies in
the answers to these questions.

The second type of variability, *within* individual variability,
is concerned with the fact that everyone's behavior varies
from time to time. Most of us have acquired many prosocial
responses; under some conditions we *perform* them, at other
times we do not. We will survey what is known about situational factors—circumstances or events that increase or
decrease the likelihood that prosocial responses will be
manifested.

Since human prosocial behavior is acquired, it can be modified. Theoretically, at least, it is possible to find ways that
parents, educators, and the media could enhance children's
prosocial behavior, thus contributing to the improvement of
the human condition, society, and the general welfare. Such
practical measures will prove to be effective, however, only if
they are based on scientific knowledge of how prosocial behavior is acquired and augmented. Such knowledge is derived
from systematic research.

A Brief Historical Note
and a Word of Warning

Trends in the behavioral sciences—the issues and questions
investigated or theorized about—are linked with social and

historical events as well as with the general temper of the times (*zeitgeist*). As citizens, many behavioral scientists are committed to the betterment of human welfare and the reduction of delinquency, injustices, prejudice, violence, and aggression. Where these concerns have been translated into empirical research, the emphasis has been on understanding actions that are clearly inimical and directly threatening to society (essentially antisocial behavior) and on providing data that can be utilized in reducing antisocial reactions. For example, it has been well established that delinquency and violence often have their roots in frustration, parental rejection, and aggressive family milieux. This information can be used in the treatment and alleviation of these social problems. Similarly, there is a substantial body of information about how tensions between groups develop and how they may be counteracted. These findings can also be applied in pragmatic social actions.

By contrast, the history of psychological research in prosocial behavior is a short one, so we know relatively little about the antecedents of altruism, charity, generosity, empathy, and compassion. Most of the studies reviewed in this book were conducted in the last fifteen or twenty years. We do not understand all the reasons for the neglect of this area of research, but we can suggest some possibilities.

First, problems that threaten to undermine the structure and functioning of the society have a quality of urgency; they demand immediate attention. Scientists are likely to become concerned with conditions that must be alleviated before they turn their attention to the promotion of positive social behavior, to kindness, consideration, and attempts to improve the general welfare. The history of medicine provides an analogy. Until the last few decades, virtually all medical research and practice was focused on the cure or control of illness, disease, and disorder. The fields of preventive medicine, emphasizing the promotion of good health, and community psychiatry, oriented toward better psychological adjustment of whole populations, developed relatively recently.

Another reason for the lag in research in prosocial behavior is inherent in the field itself; the phenomena are enormously complex and difficult to study. There are no standard methods of assessing prosocial dispositions in the sense that there are standard tests for measuring intelligence, language aptitude, learning, or problem-solving ability. To evaluate children's generosity, different investigators have used different techniques—for example, teacher's ratings, experimental or situational tests, paper and pencil tests, direct observations of naturally occurring responses (see Chapter 2, p. 15). Since these different measures are often found to be relatively independent of each other, it is difficult to identify the best or most representative criterion of prosocial behavior. Methodological problems such as these accounted in large part for the failures of early studies of prosocial behavior. For example, the Character Education Inquiry of the late 1920s[10] yielded few substantial findings but concluded that schoolchildren's cooperation and generosity are quite specific rather than general. Children were not found to be consistently cooperative or generous; rather they varied their behavior as situations changed. This study, which was extensive, costly, and widely publicized, highlighted the difficulties of studying prosocial conduct and thus had the effect of discouraging rather than stimulating further research on these critical social issues.

The last fifteen years have witnessed an upsurge of research interest in prosocial conduct, undoubtedly related to a change in the spirit of the times. Somehow the general public became more aware of the long-standing injustices suffered by women, members of minority groups, and homosexuals, and this awareness awakened sensitivity. Also, American participation in the Vietnam war led to a diversity of activist protest movements, liberalization of laws, and wider acceptance of humane values. In this atmosphere, behavioral scientists concentrated more of their efforts on trying to understand the growth and enhancement of humane attitudes and behavior.

One particular, unusual dramatic event also helped instigate a considerable number of relevant investigations of helping behavior. One night in March 1964 a young woman named Kitty Genovese was fatally stabbed in the parking lot near her apartment in Queens, New York. There were thirty-eight witnesses who heard her screams and saw her murdered but none of them did anything to help; no one called the police until the woman was dead. Excellent press coverage of this episode shocked many people into a realization of how apathetic or unconcerned with each other people can be. This in turn spurred some prominent social psychologists to initiate research and to formulate theories about why people help, or refrain from helping, others in distress.

Although interest in prosocial research has expanded substantially in recent years, there are still very complex and troublesome problems regarding methods of investigation (see also p. 18). Furthermore, the findings of some studies are contrary to the findings of others. All these things make it very difficult to synthesize research findings and to arrive at general conclusions.

The reader is therefore warned from the outset that there are numerous questions for which we do not yet have definite, dependable answers; there are fewer solutions than problems. The goal of this book is a modest one: to survey the best research on prosocial development that has been completed, to show how this research is conducted (examining both the advantages and limitations of various approaches), and to draw reasonable conclusions with the explicit acknowledgment that, in some cases, these are tentative. Since we are primarily concerned with *development*, we will concentrate on studies of children, citing some studies of adults that have clear developmental implications. What we present is the "state of the art" of research on the development of prosocial behavior, and we will highlight the areas in which more substantial data are lacking and urgently needed. By doing this, we hope to stimulate interest in this domain, inviting others to pursue further scholarship and investigation.

Some Methodological Problems and Theoretical Considerations

The form and content of acts of caring, sharing, and helping are shaped by a host of antecedents (age, personality characteristics, motivations, capabilities, judgments, ideas, and the immediate contexts encountered, to name some of them) and the intricate interactions among them. No single investigation, no matter how extensive and well designed, could possibly explore all, or even a substantial proportion, of the determinants of any form of prosocial behavior. Understandably, the immense difficulties of untangling the major consequents of each of these many factors has discouraged many competent researchers from working in this one area. Yet, in spite of the many grave difficulties, a small, vigorous, and devoted band of researchers have made, and continue to make, some progress. These researchers approach their problems in the only way possible: by selecting one (or at most a few) of the potentially significant antecedents at a time and investigating its (their) contribution to particular forms of prosocial behavior. The categories of antecedents that are powerful influences on the acquisition and development of prosocial behavior are discussed later in this chapter, and the following chapters of the book contain surveys of what is known about the variables subsumed in each of these categories.

Before proceeding, we must examine how research on prosocial behavior is conducted. The first issue is *operational definitions,* the actual behavior the investigator observes when assessing prosocial actions or predispositions. Since various operational definitions, and consequently diverse measures, of prosocial behavior are used, questions about the stability, consistency, and generality of the criteria inevitably arise. Investigators working in this domain, especially those concentrating on the processes underlying the development of prosocial responses, are seldom interested only in a limited set of observations or in transient reactions to a specific situation. Rather, they are concerned with more general and salient personal attributes or social orientations, that is, with traits or states. An investigator's measures are meaningful if they are *representatives* of *classes* or *categories* of behavior, signs or indices of stable and enduring predispositions. We will discuss this problem of representativeness, consistency, and generality of measures in the next section of this chapter.

Another section of this chapter deals with theoretical issues. In the ideal paradigm of scientific discovery, theory and hypotheses serve as guidelines for empirical investigation. But, as might be anticipated, there are no existing theories that take into account all facets and forces determining this kind of behavior, nor is it likely that such a theory will be formulated soon. We will discuss the significant contributions of three major (or "grand") psychological theories—psychoanalysis, social learning, and Piagetian theory—in this domain. Each offers insights into different aspects of prosocial development, focusing on specific, distinctive dimensions that are critical to the understanding of the issue. But no theory encompasses all the relevant variables or is capable of explaining adequately all facets of prosocial behavior.

The final section of the chapter delineates a framework for classifying the vast number of potentially significant determinants or antecedents of prosocial behavior. Categories are defined and used to organize the surveys of the empirical literature that constitute subsequent chapters of the book.

Methods of Assessing Prosocial Behavior

Although standard tests are available for measuring many psychological functions—for example, special capabilities (mechanical, mathematical) and personality characteristics (self-confidence and the need for achievement)—there are no generally accepted methods of assessing traits such as generosity, kindness, sympathy, concern for others, or altruism. Investigators therefore devise their own criterion measures or adopt them from others' research. Practically all relevant assessment techniques fall into one of the four categories described in the following paragraphs.

Situational tests consist of controlled settings designed to elicit prosocial responses. In a typical situational test of children's willingness to act generously or to share, children are first observed while playing a game, performing a task, or solving a puzzle. The participants win some prizes, such as pennies, candies, or coupons that can be redeemed for toys, and later each has an opportunity to donate some of these earnings to another child or to a charity fund for "poor or-phans." Does the child refuse to donate, give only meager amounts, or share generously? The predisposition to help someone in distress can also be tapped by means of situational tests. For example, while playing a game, the child may hear a cry of distress coming from next door. Or another child or an adult (a confederate of the experimenter's) may come into the room where the child is playing, bump her head or hurt herself in some other way, drop some papers, or express a need for help. How does the participant in the study react—with attempts to give assistance of sympathy, or by ignoring the other's plight?

It is possible, with some ingenuity, to devise situational tests to evaluate many forms of prosocial behavior. Responses in a situational test provide only a small sample of the child's behavior, but investigators generally assume that this is a *representative* sample of behavior, an indication of the child's customary or usual way of responding. This assumption can be checked by examining the relationships between perfor-mance in the particular situational test and in other settings that tap the same class of prosocial behaviors (generosity, sharing).

Ratings are used to assess the participant's standing on a continuum from high to low in an attribute such as kindness, generosity, consideration, or helpfulness. Ratings are usually made by teachers or others who know the children well and have observed their behavior frequently and in a variety of situations. In our view, such ratings are most meaningful in research with young children. Nursery school teachers observe their pupils closely and repeatedly under many different con-ditions and in spontaneous, free play situations. However, teachers in the upper grades ordinarily observe their students in relatively structured, formal classroom settings rather than in spontaneous social interactions; consequently, they are probably less able than nursery school teachers to make valid ratings of prosocial characteristics.

Sociometric questionnaires provide information about children's reputations with their peers for kindness, consideration, and other forms of prosocial conduct. The questionnaires, which are typically administered to all the students in a class, may ask the children to name their classmates who best fit certain descriptions. For example, in a number of studies of Martin Hoffman and his colleagues (see p. 93), children listed the names of three classmates who were most likely to "consider other kids' feelings" and "to help another kid who is being picked on." Of course, the sociometric questions can focus on diverse forms of prosocial behavior such as consideration, helping in emergencies, or generosity. The number of nominations received is a score or index of the child's standing in these characteristics. These sociometric assessments or peer nominations seem particularly appropriate for assessing the prosocial dispositions of children in elementary school. Children of this age probably know most of their classmates reasonably well and can therefore evaluate their typical social relationships better than their teachers can. There is, however, some danger of prejudice or "halo effect" in children's responses to questionnaires. Participants are likely to name their friends, or popular or intelligent classmates, for the favorable (prosocial) descriptions even when these are not accurate appraisals of the nominees' characteristics. Careful instructions may help to minimize this possibility.

Naturalistic observations, focused on children's behavior in their "natural" environments, may be made in playgrounds, classrooms, nursery schools, clubhouses, and parks while children go about their usual activities. No attempt is made to control or manipulate the situation, but the investigator predetermines the classes of behavior to be observed and defines them precisely (helping others in distress, giving suggestions, sharing toys, defending children being picked on, sympathizing with children who have hurt themselves). An observer systematically records all manifestations of these responses during specified observation periods, say, five minutes, on a number of occasions. Frequency of occurrence of responses is the subject's score in each category.

Naturalistic observation takes a great deal of time and effort, but, in our opinion, it is likely to provide a highly dependable and accurate estimate of the child's propensities to behave prosocially. As we shall see later, many measures of prosocial behavior based on naturalistic observations are consistent and stable over time.

Whatever method, or combination of methods, an investigator uses can assess only a small *sample* of behavior. Is this an accurate index of stable and enduring personality structures, traits, or general predispositions underlying prosocial conduct? This brings us to a critical issue of the relationship between the behaviors sampled and other manifestations or prosocial orientations—the demonstration of "major cross-situational consistencies in behavior . . .".[1] In our opinion, the accumulated evidence lends substantial support to the so-called consistency (trait or state) hypothesis with respect to prosocial characteristics. The findings of a number of studies make it clear that various measures of prosocial behavior are in fact significantly and positively incorrelated.

The Consistency and Generality of Prosocial Behavior

One of the most discouraging findings of the Hartshorne and May study of the late 1920s was the finding that moral behavior shifted from situation to situation.[2] Cheating in a test did not predict dishonesty in another situation (for example, when a storekeeper gave too much change after a purchase).

> Honesty appears here and there, or in some cases everywhere, but the 'everywheres' are exceedingly few and in view of the scattering of all the results they appear to be more reasonably explained in most cases in terms of many specific honesties. An individual cheats in one situation; the situation is slightly changed, or perhaps we should say changed in a way that seems to be slight, and the individual is now honest.[3]

The opinion that moral responses, including prosocial actions, were specific habits rather than generalized predispositions was widely accepted after the publication of this work. But more recent, reliable evidence seems to lead to an opposite conclusion. There appear to be some consistent and durable general traits or predispositions to prosocial behavior. About fifteen years ago, R. V. Burton reanalyzed the original Hartshorne and May data with the more sophisticated statistical techniques of factor analysis and concluded that there was indeed a general underlying trait of honesty, although not a very strong one, as well as specific components in the honesty tests.[4]

Subsequently, a number of other investigations have demonstrated generality of prosocial behavior, discovering predominantly positive and significant, although not always high, correlations among prosocial measures. This is especially true when these measures are based on naturalistic observations or situations, and global indices (indices composed of several measures). Assessments derived from contrived, artificial situations such as highly limited situational tests are less frequently found to correlate highly with other indices.

Let us look first at some relevant findings from studies of young children. In one, the generosity of four-year-old boys was measured by the number of candies they shared with a friend, and they were independently rated by their nursery school teachers. Those who were generous in the situational test were rated high in generosity and kindness and low in competitiveness as compared with non-generous boys.[5] Analyses of the data from naturalistic observations in a nursery school showed that nurturance and cooperative behaviors were highly correlated among the boys, and moderately correlated (correlations approaching statistical significance) among girls.[6] Another study of preschool and primary school children yielded more equivocal results: scores on experimental measures of sharing were found to be significantly correlated with the scores on comforting others, although neither of these two scores was significantly related to helping behavior.[7]

As part of an extensive longitudinal study, five-year-olds were given an opportunity to share prizes they had earned by performing a task with another child who did not have time to finish the task and had therefore not earned prizes. Those who responded generously had been described by their nursery school teachers the year before as generous, helpful and cooperative, empathic, considerate, dependable, and responsible. Those who were stingy in sharing had previously been described as aggressive and unable to delay gratification. The patterns of associations among these independently derived measures, taken at different times, are clearly congruent with the hypothesis that tendencies to prosocial actions are consistent, general, and enduring.[8]

Among seven-year-olds, measures of generosity (donations to a charity) and indices of helping behavior (the amount of work done for a peer) have been found to be significantly positively intercorrelated.[9] Furthermore, scores in two donation tasks, one involving candy and one involving money, were highly correlated in a group of five- to seven-year-olds[10] and donations in the laboratory were predictive of charity in a classroom setting.[11]

A composite score on six- and seven-year-olds' naturally occurring altruism—incidents of offering help, offering support, and making responsible suggestions to others—was highly correlated with an independently derived teacher rating of the children's overall altruism. Measures of egoistic behavior such as dominance-seeking were negatively correlated with this measure of altruism.[12] In addition, the frequency of acts of "offering help," "offering support," and "suggesting responsibly" were significantly intercorrelated in the data derived from a cross-cultural study that made use of naturalistic observations. These characteristics were found to be negatively related to egoistic behaviors[13] (see also p. 60).

Age changes in relationships among altruistic activities were noted in a study in which seven-year-olds and eleven-year-olds donated tokens to a charity, shared candy with a friend, and competed. For both ages combined, generosity to a friend was significantly positively related to charitableness and negatively related to competitiveness. However, the relationship between the two generosity measures was insignificant for the seven-year olds but substantial for those who were eleven.[14]

Three measures of prosocial behavior were collected on two groups of preadolescents, fifth- and eighth-grade pupils: a score on "other-centeredness" (assigning greater importance to values such as "having a world of equal opportunity for all people, races, and religions" than to values such as "living a life of pleasure and comfort"), sociometric measures (peer nominations for kindness and considerateness), and actual donations to charitable organizations. The three measures were significantly intercorrelated in both age groups, and some of the correlations were high.[15]

Impressive evidence of cross-situation consistency (generality) and the stability of prosocial behavior comes from a
longitudinal study that began with extensive and intensive
observations of nursery school boys and girls.[16] During the first
observational period, nurturance and sympathy to other
children, thoughtfulness, and understanding the viewpoints
of peers were all related in ways that suggested an underlying
predisposition to social responsibility and altruism. The same
boys and girls were systematically observed again in elementary school five or six years later. Again at this time, socially
responsible and altruistic behaviors were associated with each
other. Most striking from the point of view of across-time
consistency or stability were the correlations between behavior indicative of social responsibility and altruism during the
nursery school period and comparable behavior (independently observed) five or six years later ($r = .60$ for boys and $r
= .36$ for girls).[17]

It should also be noted that the correlations reported in the
studies of cross-situational consistency are *minimal* estimates—
probably actually *underestimates*—of the "true" or "real" correlations among the various criteria of particular forms of prosocial behavior. This is true for several reasons. First of all,
each criterion measure has some inherent unrealiability (error) that tends to attenuate the intercorrelations. Furthermore, when children's reactions to situational tests are used as
indices of such traits as generosity or altruism, it is assumed
that they interpret the situation as the investigators do. This
may be an unwarranted assumption, because children may
perceive the situation as demanding conformity to the experimenter's expectation. The reactions of these children may
reflect the strength of their tendencies to conform rather than
their predispositions to generosity or altruism. If this is so,
responses in the contrived situation may have no connection

with generosity in natural settings. We can expect to find ". . . evidence of cross-situational consistency only if the individuals in the research sample agree with the investigator's *a priori* claim that the sample behaviors and situations belonged in a common equivalent class. . . ."[18]

The degree of generality or consistency of prosocial responses also depends to a considerable extent on the *salience* of prosocial orientations to the participants. Bem and Allen showed that individuals who regard a trait as highly salient for them are likely to behave more consistently with respect to this trait in diverse situations, while others are more likely to vary their behavior as external circumstances change.[19] It may therefore be inferred that children who regard altruism (or generosity) as a very important personal characteristic will act consistently across situations in which altruism is elicited; those for whom altruism is less salient will vary their reactions from situation to situation, acting altruistically in some situations but not in others.

Unfortunately, very little is known about children's ordering or classification of prosocial situations, the meanings they attach to their moral responses, or the personal salience of prosocial attributes. It seems predictable, however, that investigations in which data on these factors were available and taken into account would discover higher correlations among criteria or measures of generosity or altruism.

In conclusion, according to the bulk of the evidence, children's prosocial dispositions show appreciable degrees of both consistency across situations and stability over time. Some of the obtained correlations are high, others are moderate (generally in the .30s and .40s). Although, not all studies have yielded significant cross-situational consistencies,[20] the *pattern* of findings has been replicated often and the reported correlations probably underestimate the "true" relationships between measures. The closest associations between criteria are discerned in studies using measures of the most relevant kind, that is, naturalistic observations or composite scores based on a battery of tasks.[21] The findings are congruent with the theoretical position that there are fundamental and lasting prosocial dispositions residing in individuals as general traits or states. This position is strengthened by the fact that diverse forms of prosocial response (sharing and helping) are associated with similar learning or socialization experiences (parental modeling, identification, or the use of reasoning in child rearing). We will elaborate on this later on (see Chapter 6, p. 74).

Some Theoretical Explanations of the Development of Prosocial Disposition

Given these consistencies in responses, investigators are certain to inquire about the processes underlying the acquisition and development of basic prosocial predispositions. Some pertinent hypotheses have been derived from three predominant or "grand" theories or approaches to human behavior—"grand" in the sense that they embrace diverse phenomena and incorporate many interrelated hypotheses. Each of these theories contains distinctive explanatory concepts that have implications for moral development, including prosocial conduct. We shall summarize those aspects of each theory that are most pertinent to the investigation and understanding of children's prosocial behavior.

Psychoanalytic Theory

According to psychoanalytic theory there are three major "structures" or systems of personality. The *id,* the oldest and most primitive of the systems, is composed of innate, instinctual, irrational impulses, particularly aggression and sexual desires. The primary function of the id is to gratify these impulses and to maintain a tension-free state in the organism. The *ego,* the organized, rational part of personality, develops early and acts as an intermediary between the id and the external world. It copes with reality, protects the individual against the dangers of the external world, and provides a rational, socially acceptable means of dealing with the tensions produced by the needs of the *id.* The ego governs the individual's relationship to society, and its functions include thinking, perceiving, learning, remembering, and reasoning.

The third structure, the one most relevant for understanding prosocial behavior, is the *superego,* the internalized representative of morality and the arbiter of moral conduct. This structure, which reflects the standards of society and strives for perfection, develops out of the ego, at about five or six years of age when the child resolves the Oedipus complex (the boy's sexual desire for his mother and the girl's sexual desire for her father). Then, identification with the parents replaces the mixed love, jealous, hostile, and rivalrous feelings toward them. Through identification, the child incorporates and internalizes some of the parent's (or other model's) complex patterns of behavior, personal traits and characteristics, motives, moral standards, values, and prohibitions. The superego, a major product of identification, contains two subsystems, the *conscience* and the *ego ideal.* The latter sets the moral standards or ideals, the goals aspired to, whereas the conscience judges and regulates the individual's behavior, punishes transgressions through guilt, and suppresses or redirects instinctual drives which, if acted upon, would violate the moral codes the child has internalized.

> The parents or, more precisely, their qualities as punishing and rewarding figures in the early life of the child, are introjected

into the ego and become a separate institution, the superego, which performs the same functions as the parents once did. The punishing qualities of the parents become the conscience and the rewarding qualities become the ego ideal. When the ego does not live up to the expectations of the ego ideal, conscience punishes the ego by making it feel guilty. When the ego does manage to fulfill the ideals of the superego, it is rewarded by feelings of pride.[22]

In the view of Freudian or classical psychoanalytic theory, human behavior is impelled largely by self-gratifying motives. Instinctual drives and guilt are major determinants of behavior, including social conscience, justice, and moral behavior. Freud asserted that "social justice means that we deny ourselves many things so that others may have to do without them as well, or what is the same, they may not be able to ask for them. This demand for equality is the root of social conscience and the sense of duty."[23] Guilt, self-destruction, sexual strivings, and conflict about homosexuality are the fundamental forces underlying generosity and altruism.[24]

Some more recent psychoanalytic theorists, called ego psychologists, stress the dominant role of ego processes, rather than instincts, in the formation of personality and the development of morality. They reject the notion that moral behavior and values simply represent the internalization of parental and societal values at the ages of five and six, and regard identification and moral development as ongoing, creative processes that extend into adolescence and adulthood.

> From what he is—more or less angry, demanding, aspiring, loving, anxious; from what the parents do—display certain principles in their own actions (or not), punish, espouse, love or reject; as seen through the framework of a given structure of self and a given intellectual stage; from all these, the child, over a period of years, transforms himself in new directions . . . . The acquisition of conscience and moral standards is, thus, a part of

the more general process of self or ego development; a process characterized by the creative, stage-wise, transformation of self through the internalization of new roles.[25]

Furthermore, although the parents may contribute the primary content of the child's ego ideal, subsequent identifications with "significant others" (teachers, ministers, peers) are also influential. Many changes in moral orientations, values, and attitudes, accompany the maturation of the ego structure—changes from fear to security, from aggression to tolerance and love, from moral inhibition to spontaneous kindness and consideration, and from heteronomy (use of external standards and authorities in making moral decisions) to autonomy.[26]

Psychoanalytic theory has proven to be a rich source of hypotheses about the development of shame and guilt as well as the internalization of prohibitions. However, because of its emphasis on the self-seeking aspects of human behavior, psychoanalysis cannot readily account for the development of altruistic predispositions or humanistic values (which are explained in terms of defense mechanisms and reaction formations). Nevertheless, this theory has sensitized behavioral scientists to many factors that are critical in understanding the origins and modification of prosocial orientations. One is the enduring effects of early training and experiences in shaping later behavior. Another is the role of identification, a concept formulated and introduced by Freud, but adopted (often with some changes) into practically all personality theories. In our view, identification is of utmost importance in the internalization of humanistic values and patterns of prosocial behavior, as well as in the incorporation of parental and societal prohibitions, which classical psychoanalysis stressed. If parents are nurturant, generous, and altruistic, their children may adopt these characteristics through identification.

Research on identification (and its experimental analog, modeling) and prosocial behavior will be reviewed in a later chapter (see Chapter 6, pp. 79–85).

Social Learning Theory

In contrast to psychoanalytic theory in which internal (and often unconscious) motives, emotions, instincts, and identifications predominate, social learning theory emphasizes the acquisition and development of overt responses. Social learning theorists maintain that most human behavior is learned, molded, and shaped by environmental events, especially rewards, punishments, and modeling. Essentially, the processes and mechanisms underlying animals' and humans' acquisition of a wide variety of responses, including fears, social skills, aggression, and conformity, are also invoked to explain the development of moral standards and behavior. Conscience, for example, is defined in learning theory terms as a "conditioned anxiety response to certain types of situations and actions"[27] established through the pairing of punishment or other aversive stimulation with disapproved responses such as hitting another child. As a result, the pain and anxiety associated with punishments is associated with the forbidden act and

> ... anxiety (conditioned fear) ... gradually become[s] the conditioned response to carrying out or even contemplating the naughty action, and ... this immediate negatively reinforcing consequence would discourage both contemplation and execution of the action in question. This conditioned anxiety is experienced by the child as "conscience." The acquisition of this "conscience" is, of course, facilitated by labeling, as is its generalization over different types of actions. By calling a variety of actions bad, evil, or naughty, we encourage the child to identify

them all in one category, and to react in the future with anxiety to everything thus labeled. This, very briefly and not altogether adequately, is my account of the growth of "conscience."[28]

Prosocial responses are interpreted ,as the consequents of direct reinforcements (rewards) while "moral character" is defined as learned habits and virtues that are inculcated by parents and teachers.[29] It is easy to demonstrate that if a child is rewarded by praise, attention, or gifts for sharing possessions or helping someone in distress, these responses will be strengthened, and the likelihood of the child's sharing or helping on subsequent occasions is increased. But how can reward learning account for self-sacrifice, helping, and generosity when these are not followed by any apparent reinforcements? Indeed, most prosocial actions appear to be controlled by the individual rather than by extrinsic rewards. "The assumption is that controls were originally external (through the administration of rewards and punishments by an external agent), but that behavior becomes independent of these external sanctions, and the individual comes to administer his own rewards and punishments."[30] As a consequence of repeated experiences, the children learn which responses bring parental praise, and they begin to praise themselves for these reinforced actions.

The principles of conditioning and learning have been used to explain the development of empathy (matching one's own feelings and emotions with someone else's) and of tendencies toward altruism. In one study, children in an experimental group formed a conditioned association between feelings of pleasure and the experimenter's expressions of delight. This was accomplished in the following way. The child sat close to the experimenter who demonstrated the operation of a choice box with two levers. If she pressed one lever, candy was dis-

pensed; if she pressed the other a red light flashed. The experimenter displayed no emotion when she received candy
from the box, but each time the red light flashed, she
exclaimed loudly, smiled at the child, and then hugged her.
With repeated experiences, the child's feelings of pleasure
(evoked by the experimenter's smiles, hugs, and affection)
became associated with the experimenter's rejoicing in reaction to the flash of red light. Children in control groups were
exposed to *either* the experimenter's expressions of delight
when the red light flashed *or* her affectionate responses
(smiling and hugging), but not both. Hence, for the controls,
feelings of pleasure were not attached to the experimenter's
emotional responses.

Later, each child had an opportunity to operate the choice
box while the experimenter sat on the other side of the table.
Now each participant had to choose between pressing the
lever that produced the red light that pleased the experimenter so much or pressing the lever that brought candy. In
essence, the child could obtain a material reward for herself *or*
make the experimenter happy. The majority of the children in
the experimental group pressed the lever that activated the
light more frequently than they pressed the other one, thus
sacrificing the candy reward. In contrast, the control subjects
typically pressed the candy-producing lever. As a result of
temporal contiguity and conditioning, the cues that communicated the experimenter's feelings of happiness had become capable of arousing corresponding emotions in the
children. Consequently, the investigator asserted, they were
motivated to produce signs of pleasure in the experimenter.
The cues originally associated with direct, external rewards
(smiling, hugging) gradually acquired a cognitive, internal
representation and thus were able to exercise control over
behavior.[31]

Observational Learning. No developmental psychologist would argue against the assertion that direct rewards facilitate the learning of prosocial behavior. But it is also clear that a substantial proportion of the individual's helping and sharing responses is acquired through observation and imitation of a model's behavior, without direct reinforcements. The pioneering work of Bandura and Walters on observational learning and imitation[32] stimulated a great deal of theorizing and research that has proven highly salient in the investigation of prosocial behavior. Bandura maintains identification with the parent is operationally identical with the child's imitation of parental responses. In Chapter 6, on socialization in the family, we shall examine the modeling and identification as critical antecedents of prosocial predispositions (see pp. 74-100).

Social learning theory has many profound implications for the study of early socialization, including the socialization of prosocial behavior. According to Eleanor Maccoby,

> Whether one emphasizes modeling or direct reinforcement or both, the parents ... play a crucial role in the socialization process for any social-learning theorist, for the parents serve as the most consistently available and salient models as well as the primary dispensers of reinforcement during the early part of the child's life. Furthermore, although a child may *acquire* elements of social behavior through observation of a model with whom he is not directly interacting, the *performance* of the behavior tends to be controlled by the immediate reinforcement contingencies; hence the people who are in a position to control these contingencies will have the greatest effect on what the child *does,* even if they have less exclusive control over what he learns how to do. The parents, then, are the central figures in early socialization, and this makes them central for the whole of moral development, for in social-learning theory, early learned behavior tends to persist. Behavior once learned will be maintained unless the reinforcement contingencies are changed. There is no inner

programming producing change as there is in the cognitive-developmental approach. Stability of behavior tends to be maintained by the tendency of the individual to seek or stay in environments which will not demand change of him. Therefore, socialization during early childhood is of great importance for the social-learning theorist, and much of the research stemming from this point of view has dealt with the preschool child and the effects upon him of variations in parental socialization practices.[33]

Cognitive Developmental Theory

The cognitive-developmental theorist's conceptualization of the nature of development contrasts sharply with those of psychoanalytic and social learning theorists. Children are not seen as passive, driven by instinctive impulses, or shaped by environmental forces. Rather, they *act on* the environment, often in creative ways, just as the environment acts on them. Each perceives the environment in his or her own way, interprets and organizes stimuli, and behaves as an intelligent being. According to Piaget, intelligence, which includes all cognitive functions, serves the purpose of adaptation. Cognitive development, the result of the interaction between changing (maturing) mental structures and environmental events, proceeds through a universal, invariant sequence of stages. Each stage is an integrated whole that is qualitatively different from the others, and earlier stages are replaced and integrated into later ones. Moral reasoning and judgment, which are manifestations of intelligence, grow and change as other cognitive functions do. Cognitive development thus provides "a framework for and imposes restraints upon the nature of the moral judgments that are possible for children of different ages."[34]

Proponents of cognitive developmental theory are not primarily concerned with moral *behavior*, or with the motives or affects that regulate prosocial actions. Both Piaget and Kohlberg have described stages in the development of moral reasoning and judgment. (These will be discussed in Chapter 8, see pp. 109–138). They explicitly recognize that moral thought, as they define and measure it, may not always correspond to actions. But Kohlberg asserts, "The fact that children do not always do what they say when the chips are down does not mean that development of judgment and development of conduct go along two different tracks. Verbal judgment may not be 'trustworthy' reports of conduct, but they may still reflect the same basic developmental process."[35]

In our view, the cognitive developmental theorists have contributed immensely to the understanding of morality and of the development of prosocial behavior by illuminating the nature of age changes in moral judgments and role-taking ability. As will become clearer, moral behavior is related to maturity of moral judgment and to cognitive skills such as role-taking (see pp. 124–138).

The Determinants of Prosocial Behavior

None of these major theories can adequately handle all facets of prosocial development. The three approaches deal with different aspects of moral behavior; each has its own emphases and conceptualizations of the basic mechanisms underlying moral and prosocial development. Yet each makes unique contributions to our understanding of this multifaceted problem by stressing distinctive critical antecedents.

There are also some points of agreement in the three approaches. According to all three theories, children are initially self-centered (egocentric, in the cognitive-developmental theorists' terms), becoming more oriented toward others as they achieve greater cognitive maturity and gain more experience. Concomitantly, the control of moral behavior shifts from external rewards and punishments (by parental or other authorities) to internalized motives or individualized principles.

Each theory complements the others by centering attention on aspects of prosocial behavior that the other theories underplay or neglect. Cognitive developmental theory underscores the significance of thinking, reasoning, judging, and role-taking—all functions that are underplayed in psychoanalytic and social learning theory. Psychoanalytic theory, on the other hand, stresses the critical roles of emotions and motives, early parent–child relationships, and identification, and all of these are fundamental in the development of prosocial behavior (see pp. 85–92).

Each of the three theories has generated a great deal of relevant research, but social learning theory has probably been the most fruitful source of hypotheses about the development of prosocial behavior. This is due to its focus on overt responses and the reformulation of psychoanalytic concepts into learning terms. The impact of social learning theory on empirical research will be apparent throughout this book.

Since no existing theory can handle all the central issues of the formation and development of prosocial characteristics, our approach is frankly pluralistic, reflecting the enormous complexity of this domain of behavior. We are fully aware that we must deal with many subtle, interacting antecedents. We do not propose a new theory, but we will proceed with orderly and systematic analyses of the major classes of determinants of prosocial behavior, and review relevant studies of the impacts of various determinants. Many of these investigations were guided by theory or were specifically designed to test theoretical hypotheses dealing, for example, with identification, originally a psychoanalytic concept (see p. 79), or empathy, a concept closely related to role-playing, which is of central importance in cognitive developmental theory (see pp. 126–138).

Existing theories do not encompass all facets of prosocial behavior, so they are not the only source of research hypotheses in this field. Many empirical questions originate from the following: a priori, rational analyses of the components and antecedents of prosocial actions; "minitheories" that deal with restricted issues such as empathy (see p. 127); observations of children's spontaneous interactions with parents and peers; common sense; folk wisdom. To illustrate, "folk wisdom" says that child-rearing practices have strong impacts on the child's behavior and attitudes. Different ways of handling discipline (harsh punishment, exhortation or preaching, reasoning and explanation) may be expected to have different effects on children's predispositions to prosocial behavior. These issues are obviously important, certainly worthy of investigation, yet none of the three major theories deals extensively with these variables. (The principles of social learning theory, however, may be applied in formulating hypotheses about these differential effects.)

In brief, to achieve deeper understanding of the acquisition and development of prosocial behavior, we can be guided by psychoanalytic, social learning, or cognitive developmental theories. But our thinking and research should not be restricted by these. We must also examine other kinds of theories, speculations, and empirical studies concerned with critical issues and variables not included in these major developmental theories.

Categories of Determinants

What are the determinants or antecedents of prosocial behavior? It is at least possible that *biological factors* play a role, and some have speculated that these are genetic predispositions to act altruistically. It is well established that this is the case for certain subhuman species, and we will review some fascinating and thought-provoking comparative studies of altruism in Chapter 3. It is tempting to generalize from some of the exciting findings in studies of animals about the biological bases of human prosocial behavior, but, as we shall see, such generalizations may be unwarranted. Tentatively, however, we will consider *biological factors* as a category of determinants.

A vast number of other factors have potentials for making significant impacts on prosocial behavior in humans; any particular prosocial action is determined by many complex factors. These fall into four major categories: group membership or culture; socialization experiences, primarily within the family; cognitive functions; situational conditions and circumstances.

We alluded to the category *group membership and culture* at the beginning of this book by contrasting the selfish and, from the point of view of Western culture, ruthless behavior of the Ik with the traditionally high levels of the Hopi Indians' cooperativeness and consideration of others. It is an accepted fact that people's actions, motives, orientations, and values are, to an appreciable degree, governed by the cultures in which they are reared. All aspects of behavior and psychological functioning that are acquired rather than inherited "have—at least in their more superficial and peripheral aspects—a cultural tinge."[36]

But membership in a cultural group can account only for general tendencies; it cannot explain individual variations within cultures in propensities to act prosocially. In discussing the cultural determinants of personality, Kluckhohn and Murray make statements that apply equally well to the determination of individual differences in prosocial behavior.

> If there were no variations in the conceptions and applications of cultural standards, personalities [or predispositions to act prosocially] formed in a given society would be more nearly alike than they actually are. Culture determines only what an individual learns as a member of a group—not so much what he learns as a private individual and as a member of a particular family. Because of these special experiences and particular constitutional endowments, each person's selection from and reaction to cultural teachings have an individual quality. . . . Deviation from cultural norms is inevitable and endless. . . .[37]

The category of determinants labeled *socialization experiences,* the "special experiences" referred to in the quotation above, encompasses all the child's interactions with the major agents of socialization such as parents (the most significant agents), peers, teachers, and the mass media. Evaluating the accumulated empirical data on the influences of these socialization experiences, we have concluded that the events subsumed by this category are most critical in molding the child's prosocial predispositions.

The next category, *cognitive functions* or level of cognitive maturity, includes variables that loom large in cognitive developmental theory: perceptions, interpretations and evaluations of situations; level of cognitive development or maturity;

intelligence; the ability to see and evaluate the situation from the perspective of others (role-taking); attitudes; and decision-making processes. All these factors affect the child's prosocial attributes and actions.

These classes of determinants relate to deep-lying personality traits, motives, and cognitive capabilities that help regulate children's prosocial responses. But, external pressures, social events, and social contexts also may be powerful determinants. The category *situational determinants* embraces two different kinds of events. The first refers to events that "just happen" to the individual—for instance, chance or casual encounters that have enduring effects, influencing an entire life course, impelling the individual to become altruistic or mean. The second subcategory of situational determinants has to do with the immediate social context, the situation or circumstance confronting the individual. Included are relatively transient emotions, feelings, or moods, as well as short-lived social interactions.

The rest of this book is devoted to surveys, syntheses, and evaluations of the empirical evidence about each of these categories of determinants of prosocial behavior. A few more words are needed before proceeding, however. It must be recognized that these determinants are not independent; they are, in fact, interdependent, interacting, and linked in intricate and complex ways. This is very easily demonstrated. The cultural milieu in which children are reared sets constraints on their socialization experiences; for example, children in some cultures are never spanked, and children in other cultures are almost never reasoned with. In most cases, the child's learning at home (socialization experiences) is congruent with, and reinforces, the norms and standards of the culture in which the child is growing up (group membership or culture). But conflict is generated if the culture stresses behavior, attitudes, and values that differ from those taught at home, and this conflict is likely to affect the development of prosocial behavior.

Socialization experiences undoubtedly affect cognitive functions and abilities (another category), and the latter, in turn, undoubtedly influence the child's reactions to socialization experiences. In addition, the interpretation of the immediate social context is to some extent dependent on the child's cognitive maturity and personality structure, both of which are affected by socialization experiences.

As you read further in this book, it will become clearer that it is virtually impossible to evaluate precisely the relative contributions of these various determinants to the development of helping and sharing. In our opinion, *socialization experiences* make up the most important set of determinants, but this is an opinion, not an established fact. We simply do not have the kinds of data necessary to determine whether the home environment is more important than cognitive maturity in the development of predispositions to prosocial actions.

More is known about some categories of determinants than about others, and, within categories, some determinants have been investigated more adequately than others. For reasons we do not fully understand, the effects of situational factors on helping behavior have been examined more thoroughly than the effect of cognitive variables. And, within the category *socialization experiences,* there is abundant evidence on the effects of identification with parents on prosocial predispositions but relatively little information about peer influences.

Of course, these are the kinds of discrepancies and deficiences that are to be expected in the early developmental stages of complex fields of investigation.

Biology and
Prosocial Behavior

Prosocial behavior is *not* an exclusively human achievement. Many animals below man on the phylogenetic scale, ranging from social insects (ants, termites, bees, and wasps) through such mammals as hunting dogs, elephants, and dolphins, and up to the higher primates, exhibit behaviors that are at least superficially similar to human altruism, sharing, and self-sacrifice to the benefit of the group (or species). Recently, Edward O. Wilson, a prominent biologist at Harvard University, published a much publicized, stimulating, and controversial book called *Sociobiology*.[1] It is essentially the founding work of a new scientific field dedicated to the systematic study of the biological basis of social behavior. The book is rich in examples of actions of animals that appear to be prosocial. We will sample a few of these.

Some social insects are suicidally self-sacrificing. Honeybee workers attack intruders at the hive, embedding their barbed stings in their victims. When this occurs, the bee's venom gland is pulled out and much of its viscera with it, so that it soon dies. Its attack is successful, however, because the venom gland continues to secrete poison into the intruders' wounds and the odor coming from the sting excites other members of the hive to make further attacks on the intruders. Similar self-sacrificing defensive acts occur among certain ants and wasps. "The fearsome reputation of social bees and wasps is due to their general readiness to throw away their lives upon slight provocation" in defense of their colonies.[2]

Members of many other species will also readily risk their lives to defend others, particularly their own young or their relatives. For example, the females of some bird species, such as ducks and partridges, protect their young from predators by feigning injury and acting as though they could be captured easily. When a mother bird spots a predator nearby, she acts as though her wing is broken, stumbling and fluttering at some distance (usually a safe distance) from her nest to draw the predator's attention away from the young. She moves farther from the nest, stumbling repeatedly, leading the predator away from her babies. Finally, when the predator is a safe distance from the nest the female tries to fly away. In many cases, she escapes and so do her young. However, in some cases the predator may capture her, but because of her actions, the young survive.

Certain small birds, such as robins and thrushes, warn other members of their species of an approaching predator hawk by crouching low and giving a distinctive thin reedy whistle. In doing so, they attract attention to themselves and thus run the risk of being captured and killed. The warning calls appear to be altruistic, protecting the lives of others. The caller itself would be safer, however, if it did not reveal its presence but remained silent and escaped.

Various species of animals manifest altruism by sharing food. During one season of the year, for example, packs of African wild dogs live in dens, and some adults must stay at home to guard the pups while others go out to hunt for food. When the hunters return, they give fresh meat to those who stayed at home, or regurgitate pieces for them. These actions benefit those who stayed at home with the pup, usually including the mother, as well as sick and crippled adults who are unable to hunt. Also, in this species, mother dogs sometimes allow hungry adults to suckle their milk.

According to Wilson, chimpanzees appear to be the most altruistic of all animals. These animals are ordinarily vegetarians but occasionally capture rodents, monkeys, or baboons for food. While the successful hunters dismember the prey and feast on it, other chimps may approach to beg for morsels. The hunters often respond to the beggars' appeal, permitting them to feed directly on the meat or pulling off pieces and donating these. Chimpanzees also help others by communicating the location of food or by leading others to it.

How can animal altruism, especially of the self-sacrificing sort, be explained? Wilson and other biologists explain the phenomenon by invoking the concept of *kin selection,* a broadened view of natural selection. Through self-sacrificing actions, it is argued, the animal increases the probability that its close relatives, who share its genes, will survive. Shared genes are preserved by the altruist's sacrifice and these can then be transmitted.

> In the process of natural selection . . . any device that can insert a higher proportion of certain genes into subsequent generations will come to characterize the species. One class of such devices promotes prolonged individual survival. Another promotes superior mating performance and care of the resulting offspring. As more complex social behavior by the organism is added to the genes' techniques for replicating

themselves, altruism becomes increasingly prevalent and eventually appears in exaggerated forms. This brings us to the central theoretical problem of sociobiology: how can altruism, which by definition reduces personal fitness, possibly evolve by natural selection? The answer is kinship: if the genes causing the altruism are shared by two organisms because of common descent, and if the altruistic act by one organism increases the joint contribution of these genes to the next generation, the propensity to altruism will spread through the gene pool. This occurs even though the altruist makes less of a solitary contribution to the gene pool as the price of its altruistic act.[3]

The mechanism can be shown most clearly in termite soldiers who are genetically programmed to sacrifice themselves when they attack ants and other enemies. To fight them off, the termite soldiers spray a glandular secretion that fatally entangles both themselves and their victims. By sacrificing itself, the termite soldier "protects the rest of the colony, including the queen and king which are the soldier's parents. As a result, the soldier's more fertile brothers and sisters flourish, and it is *they* which multiply the altruistic genes that are shared with the soldier by close kinship. One's own genes are multiplied by the greater production of nephews and nieces."[4]

The beneficiaries of altruism are in many cases the altruist's relatives, but many animals behave altruistically toward nonrelatives as well. Sociobiologists use the concept *reciprocal altruism* to explain this behavior. The fundamental idea is that the altruistic act entails danger (and no immediate benefit) to the altruist, but it may serve to evoke a reciprocal altruistic act by the beneficiary at some future time; that is, the altruist will sometime in the future be the target of the beneficiary's altruistic acts.[5]

Sociobiology is a fascinating account of social behavior among many groups of animals, and it provides a lucid account of evolutionary principles that may account for such behavior.

The book has generated a great deal of heated controversy, most of it centered on the final chapter of the book in which the author speculates that human social behavior, including altruistic behavior, may also be under genetic control. Wilson reasons this way: altruistic acts in animal societies can be plausibly explained as outcomes of kin selection. Humans also perform altruistic acts, so these are also likely to have a direct genetic basis. But, as critics point out, similarity of result does not imply identity of cause.

There is no doubt that humans have a biological *potential* for altruistic actions—otherwise they could not perform them. Furthermore, human altruism is often adaptive. But these facts in themselves are hardly sufficient evidence that human altruism is under direct genetic control. In fact, there is no evidence to support the notion that specific genes determine human altruistic or other prosocial behavior. Even Wilson says humans "have given away most of their sovereignty," and he has stated that he believes that perhaps ten percent of human social behavior has a genetic basis.

Stephen J. Gould, a biologist and historian of science, admires Wilson's empirical observational work but criticizes his extrapolation of the concept of genetic determinism to human social behavior. In an account of an argument he had with an eminent anthropologist, he underscores the fallacy of accepting a genetic explanation for human altruism.

> My colleague insisted that the classic story of Eskimo on ice floes provides adequate proof for the existence of specific altruist genes maintained by kin selection. Apparently, among some Eskimo peoples, social units are arranged as family groups. If food resources dwindle and the family must move to survive, aged grandparents willingly remain behind (to die) rather than endanger the survival of the entire family by slowing an ardous and dangerous migration. Family groups with no altruist genes

have succumbed to natural selection as migrations hindered by the old and sick lead to the death of entire families. Grandparents with altruist genes increase their own fitness by their sacrifice, for they insure the survival of close relatives sharing their genes.

The explanation by my colleague is plausible, to be sure, but scarcely conclusive since an eminently simple, nongenetic explanation also exists: there are no altruist genes at all, in fact, no important genetic differences among Eskimo families whatsoever. The sacrifice of grandparents is an adaptive, but nongenetic trait. Families with no tradition for sacrifice do not survive for many generations. In other families, sacrifice is celebrated in song and story; aged grandparents who stay behind become the greatest heroes of the clan. Children are socialized from their earliest memories to the glory and honor of such sacrifice.

I cannot prove my scenario, any more than my colleague can demonstrate his. But in the current context of no evidence, they are at least equally plausible. Likewise, reciprocal altruism undeniably exists in human societies, but this provides no evidence whatever for its genetic basis. As Benjamin Franklin said: "We must all hang together, or assuredly we shall all hang separately." Functioning societies may require reciprocal altruism. But these acts need not be coded into our being by genes; they may be inculcated equally well by learning.[6]

We concur with the view shared by most behavioral scientists: What humankind inherits is the potential or possibility of learning a wide variety of social behaviors. But what is actually learned depends on the social situation. Socially adaptive cooperative and altruistic behaviors are the products of social learning and not biological evolution. And social evolution is based on psychological and social mechanisms rather than genetic ones.

> Through the social mechanisms of child socialization, reward and punishment, socially restricted learning opportunities, identification, imitation, emulation, indoctrination into tribal

ideologies, language and linguistic meaning systems, conformity pressures, social authority systems, and the like . . .
sufficient retention machinery exists for a social evolution of
adaptive social belief systems and organizational principles to
have taken place.[7]

The available evidence leads us to doubt that specific genes
or other biological factors have any major role in determining
the prosocial responses of humans or individual differences in
propensities toward prosocial actions. We agree with the
eminent physical anthropologist Washburn, who asserts that
". . . the search for altruistic genes in man is as unlikely to be
rewarding as is the search for specific genes determining [the
learning of] French or German. . . . It is biology that learns,
and to emphasize learning in no way removes biological considerations. But the more learning is basic, the less will there
be any simple relationship between genes and behaviors."[8]

Culture and
Prosocial Behavior

Anthropologists describe the norms of behavior, including perceptions, cognitions, thoughts, beliefs, ideals and values, that are traditional, typical (or modal), and "expected" of people in particular cultures or subcultures. The array of cultural variation is enormous. After studying sex and temperament in a number of primitive cultures, Margaret Mead concluded that ". . . human nature is almost unbelievably malleable, responding accurately and contrastingly to contrasting cultural conditions."[1]

In many cultures, prosocial conduct predominates, whereas in others, egoistic and selfish qualities are the norm. Reflect on the sharp contrasts between the Ik and the Hopi described at the beginning of this book (see pp. 2-3). Turnbull compares the Ik with members of other hunting societies who "frequently display those characteristics that we find so admirable in man, kindness, generosity, consideration, affection, honesty, hospitality, compassion, charity. For them, in their tiny close-knit society these are necessities for survival."[2] Turnbull hypothesizes that the Ik lost these qualities when their established culture and traditions disintegrated completely because of a combination of disastrous historical, political, and technological events. After this, there was no society, or social order; membership in the group became meaningless, and the struggle for sheer existence became paramount, and self-interest completely replaced humane relationships and consideration for others.

Societies and cultures can maintain themselves only if the members have at least some concern about each other, but degree of social concern varies greatly from culture to culture. Cooperation and social responsibility are outstanding features of some cultures, but these qualities are not highly valued in others. Margaret Mead found two tribes on the same island, New Guinea,[3] with strikingly different patterns of personality and behavior. Members of one, the Arapesh, were gentle, loving, cooperative, generous, unaggressive people who were highly responsive to the needs and feelings of others and unconcerned about personal property. Mundugamor men and women, in contrast, displayed opposite characteristics; they were ruthless, aggressive, quarrelsome, undisciplined, lacking in gentleness and cooperation.

This wide range of variations is not restricted to primitive cultures. Modern societies also differ radically from each other in social orientations and interactions. For example, Israeli Kibbutz culture

> can survive only if the members of the kibbutz are highly motivated to work for the welfare of the entire society. The Sabras (native born Israelis) seem to have acquired this drive. They have learned . . . that prestige is attained primarily by behavior which benefits others. For the youngest children, who are in the

process of learning the cultural norms the most frequent response to the question [What are the things you could do for which others would praise you?] is "generosity" with either assistance or goods. For the oldest group [of children questioned] which presumably has already learned the cultural norms, the most frequent category of response is "social responsibility," i.e., doing those things from which the group as a whole will benefit.[4]

In contemporary Soviet society, cooperation and social responsibility, consideration of others and of the needs and welfare of the collective (rather than of oneself) are the most highly valued personal qualities. As we shall see, these are emphasized and inculcated by parents and all other agents of socialization, including the school and youth groups, from early infancy on (see p. 57).

Studies of cultures that differ from our own (the Hopi, the Arapesh, Ik, Israeli kibbutzim, the Soviet Union, for example) help delineate the wide spectrum of norms and of "typical" or "modal" behaviors that exists. This demonstration broadens our own perspectives and keeps us from concluding that any particular trait or motive prevalent in one culture reflects a significant fact about universal, innate, basic, biologically determined, or "raw" properties of human nature.

It is unfortunate from our point of view that few ethnographic studies focus on prosocial behaviors such as generosity, consideration, and helping. Some anthropologists have provided excellent descriptions of average or modal forms of prosocial conduct in particular cultures and offer suggestions about possible antecedents of such conduct, but they do not ordinarily collect information about the underlying psychological dynamics or processes.

Mead hypothesized, for example, that the gentle and submissive characteristics of the Arapesh stem, in large part, from the "cherishing" and tender attention Arapesh parents give their children, and Spiro attributes kibbutz children's extraordinary sense of social responsibility primarily to peer-group pressures. In this culture, peer-group approval is more important than parental approval in the socialization process, at least from the age of six on. "The Sabras, who . . . are highly sensitive to public opinion, believe that the most effective technique for acquiring the acclaim of one's fellows is to assume a large share of social responsibility. And this is exactly what is demanded in a society which has a minimum of formal leadership patterns."[6]

Mead's and Spiro's hypotheses are tenable, but the supportive evidence they offer is less than compelling. The simple fact that the two phenomena occur together in one culture (for example, a high level of social responsibility and strong peer-group pressure or consideration of others and tender care in infancy) is not evidence that one is the antecedent of the other. Testing hypotheses about antecedent–consequent relationships between two variables requires data from many cultures collected and analyzed in the same ways, and then compared. Suppose, for example, we wanted to test the hypothesis that living in a close-knit, traditional way of life was in fact more characteristic of cultures high in sharing than of the others. In this way, "anthropolotical evidence has been and can continue to be of invaluable service as a crucible in which to put to more rigorous test psychology's tentative theories, enabling one to edit them and select among alternatives in ways which laboratory experiments and correlational studies within our own culture might never make possible."[7]

Unfortunately, there are relatively few studies that test relationships in this way. The ones that are most relevant to the cross-cultural comparative study of prosocial behavior will be reviewed in this chapter.

Cooperation, Competition, and Sharing

Cultural variations in children's tendencies to cooperate or compete have been investigated systematically by Millard Madsen and his co-workers at the University of California at Los Angeles. Their data are particularly appropriate for cross-cultural comparisons because they used comparable research methods with different groups.

A number of specially devised situational tests of cooperation and competition are used in the research. One of these tests or "games" makes use of the cooperation board diagrammed in Figure 1. The board is 18 inches square and it has an eyelet at each corner. A string passes through each of the eyelets and is attached to a metal weight which serves as a holder for a ball point pen. A sheet of paper is placed on the board for each trial so that the movement of the pen as the children pull their string is automatically recorded.

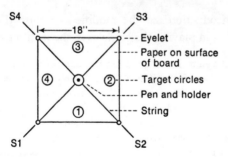

FIGURE 1. Cooperation board. (Source: A. Shapira and M. C. Madsen, "Cooperation and Competitive Behavior of Afro-American, Anglo-American, and Mexican Village Children," Developmental Psychology, 3, 1970.)

Four children play the game together and the object is to draw lines through target circles, one at each side of the square (see diagram). The string and eyelets are arranged so that each child can only pull his pen in one direction, toward himself. It is therefore practically impossible to cross a circle if any child tries to prevent it by pulling his or her own string. Children must cooperate in order to draw the lines through the circles and thus win prizes. Competition is maladaptive because no one can win if the children oppose each other in pulling the strings.

Instructions can be varied to heighten cooperation and group orientation by having only *group* rewards. The following introduction to the game accomplishes this.

> As you can see, when we pull the string the pen draws lines. In this game we are going to pull the strings and draw the lines but in a special way. The aim of the game is for you to draw a line over the four circles in one minute. If you succeed in doing this each of you will get a prize. If you cover the four circles twice, everyone will get two prizes and so on, but if you cover less than four circles, no one will get a prize. You may talk to each other but are not allowed to touch another child's string. . . .[8]

The introduction can be modified to raise the level of competition in playing the game as in the instructions

> Now the game is going to be somewhat different. Now everyone gets his own circles. This is David's circle (E. writes name on a circle to the right of David). This is Ron's circle (etc.) Now when the pen draws a line across one of the circles, the child whose name is in the circle gets a prize. When it crosses David's circle, David gets a prize; when it crosses Ron's circle, Ron gets a prize and so on. You will have one minute to play before I stop you. . . .

Under these conditions, only one child can win a reward at a time; rewards are *individual*. However, because any child can prevent another from crossing his or her own circles, the adaptive strategy is to cooperate, so that all the circles can be crossed quickly and all players can thus receive prizes.

Cooperation in these studies differs in one very important respect from the forms of prosocial behavior with which we are principally concerned. In these situational tests, cooperation is self-serving as well as helpful to others; the actor benefits as much as fellow players do. Critical components of our definition of prosocial behavior—specifically, absence of direct reward for the actions and some cost of self-sacrifice (or risk of cost)—are missing in this situation.

To appraise the extent of cultural differences in tendencies to cooperate or compete, investigators have administered this game and similar ones to children in many cultural settings. Included are children in rural traditional (generally agricultural) or communal cultures in which the way of life has been relatively unchanged over very long periods of time as well as those from cities where Western European orientations prevail, and the traditional lifestyle has been transformed substantially in the past few decades. Cross-cultural data from a number of studies reveal a consistent pattern: children reared in traditional rural subcultures and small, semiagricultural communal settlements cooperate more readily than children reared in modern urban subcultures. For example, school children in Mexican villages and small towns are far less competitive than their urban middle-class Mexican, Mexican-American, Afro-American, or Anglo-American peers.[9] Similarly, children from kibbutzim and Arab villages in Israel are more cooperative than urban Israeli children;[10] rural Columbian children of school age cooperate more than urban children in that country,[11] and New Zealand Maori children, from a traditional rural culture, are more cooperative than New Zealand, European, and urban Maori children.[12]

Children of all cultures cooperate with others if cooperation is rewarded directly, that is, when there are *group* rewards to be shared by all. However, when instructions are changed and only *individual* rewards are available, cultural differences become manifest. Canadian Blackfoot Indian children, Australian aborigines, Mexican and Columbian village children, and those from Israeli kibbutzim continue to cooperate with each other under these individual reward conditions. The kibbutz children participating in the study attempted to organize the players for cooperation, rallying the group with statements like "Let's help each other" or "Okay gang, let's go in turns" or "Let's start here, then go here, then there." Somehow being reared in a traditional culture, especially a rural one, reinforces the maintenance of high levels of cooperation even when the rewards are individual. In contrast, children living in cities—Afro- and Anglo-American, Israeli, Columbian, and Mexican—tend to compete in ineffective and maladaptive ways under these conditions.[13]

Effects of Living in Two Cultures

Those who move from the traditional cultures in which they were raised may adopt two different cultural orientations. Under these circumstances, the individual's motivations are apt to change in the direction of the dominant, urban group, that is, toward less cooperation and more competition. Thus, studies of Mexican, Mexican-American, and Anglo-American children seven to nine years old showed the Mexicans to be most cooperative and the Anglo-Americans the most competitive. The Mexican-American children who participated in both Mexican and American cultures, fell between the other two groups. These children "... are like the Anglo-Americans in refusing complete cooperation, but like the Mexicans in avoiding competition."[14]

Analogously, Australian aborigines who live in traditional aboriginal ways tend to be more cooperative than Australians of European background, but aborigines with high educational goals, and therefore greater orientation toward a European way of life, are less cooperative (more competitive) than those with low er educational objectives. In general, Canadian Indian children, particularly males, show more cooperative behavior than urban Canadians.[15] But Indians attending an integrated school, acculturated to white standards, are more competitive than Indians who have more sustained contact with traditional Indian ways. Interestingly, the white Canadians at the integrated school seemed to take on some of their Indian peers' cooperative orientation and tendencies.

Explanations of Cultural Variations in Prosocial Behavior

Given these cross-cultural data, we can hardly dispute that the culture in which the child is reared is a major force in shaping her or his dispositions toward cooperation or competition. To understand cultural differences in these tendencies, we need precise descriptions of the socialization techniques to stimulate or restrict the development of prosocial behavior. Unfortunately, we have relatively few details of child-rearing practices in other cultures. To account for cultural differences in prosocial orientations, cross-cultural investigators usually make rather vague references to socialization practices, implying that children acquire their norms, values, and behaviors by imitation and reinforcement or reward. For instance, Millard Madsen speculates that the dramatic differences in cooperation between rural and urban Mexican children are rooted in different patterns of family functioning in the two settings. In poor agricultural communities, children must cooperate in working with other members of their families to raise enough food for the family's survival. Such cooperation is rewarded because it benefits the whole family, while competitive and aggressive tendencies are punished because they threaten family unity. "Through consistent reinforcement the child learns that conflict is unacceptable and that cooperation is expected."[16] On the other hand, middle-class urban parents regard competitiveness as necessary and desirable because it is advantageous in the economic struggle for survival. They are models of competitiveness and also reinforce their children's competitive responses repeatedly. Teachers in the middle-class urban schools also reward competition more than teachers in rural schools do.

Kibbutz parents and teachers reinforce each other in inculcating cooperative values and orientations and in discouraging competition among children.

> In the kibbutz ... children are prepared from an early age to cooperate and work as a group, in keeping with the objectives of communal living. . . . Generosity and cooperation were the most frequently rewarded behaviors, while selfishness and failure to cooperate were among the behaviors most frequently punished.
>
> The formal teaching methods in the kibbutz are also noted for their minimal emphasis on competitive goals and techniques. . . . Competition, with all its punitive aspects, is far less intense in the classroom of the kibbutz than in that of the city. Not only do the agents of socialization avoid inducing a favorable set toward competition, but also the children themselves develop an attitude against competition. . . . By far the majority of the students said that their desire was primarily to become equal to their peers or . . . to raise the achievement level of their group as a whole.[17]

This is in sharp contrast to what is stressed by their counterparts in the cities who encourage their children to achieve and succeed through competition.

Analogously, the cooperativeness of Blackfoot Indian children has been attributed to traditions of sharing all material wealth, child rearing, and housekeeping duties with other members of the family. The sharply contrasting level of competition of their Canadian, non-Indian peers is alleged to result from their being raised "within the general North American cultural milieu with its support of individual competition and achievement."[18]

These explanations of cultural variations in children's tendencies to compete or cooperate, conceptualized as consequents of the norms and values of different cultures, seem plausible. However, the hypothesized links between aspects of the cultural milieu and children's prosocial conduct are not spelled out in detail, and the proposed explanations are of limited value in clarifying the psychological processes that mediate the acquisition of prosocial orientations. As Kluckhohn pointed out long ago, ". . . historical accident, environmental pressures, and seemingly immanent causation, though all important, are not adequate to explain fully the observed facts of cultural differentiation. Unless we are to assume that each distinct culture was divinely revealed to its carriers, we must have recourse to psychology as part of the process."[19] What is needed is detailed and focused examination of precisely how the norms and approved responses are communicated and inculcated, how children learn them, and how they are generalized to new circumstances. This is not to be construed as criticism of the research studies reviewed above, which successfully do what they were designed to do: They demonstrate cultural differences in cooperation and competition. They did not purport to investigate the socialization of prosocial behavior.

Socialization in the Soviet Union

One exceptional study of the socialization of prosocial orientations is worthy of special note—Urie Bronfenbrenner's multifaceted analysis of how predominant tendencies toward altruism and orientations toward the group (or collective) are inculcated in children in the Soviet Union.[20] The investigation shows clearly that the process is started in the early phases of childhood:

> From the very beginning stress is placed on teaching children to share and to engage in joint activity. Frequent reference is made to common ownership: "Moe eto nashe; nashe moe" [mine is ours; ours is mine]. Collective play is emphasized. Not only group games, but special complex toys are designed which require the cooperation of two or three children to make them work.[21]

There are virtually no discontinuities in the socialization process in the Soviet Union. On the contrary, all agents of socialization (parents, workers in preschool centers, teachers, peers, the mass media) reinforce and support each other's deliberate efforts to inculcate "Communist ideals," cooperation, and orientation toward collective living. With increasing age, children are expected to take on more and more communal responsibilities, such as helping others and sharing in the work of the schools and the broader community. The schools emphasize not only subject matter but also "character development," which includes cooperation, sharing, altruism, and consideration of the group. Youth groups and collectives of children formed within the classroom function to help maintain discipline and further encourage a collective orientation. "In Communist schools, a deliberate effort is made— through appropriate models, reinforcements, and group experiences—to teach the child the values and *behaviors* consistent with Communist ideals."[22]

Bronfenbrenner's study is unique in illuminating in detail the techniques and pressures used in one complex culture to instill a definite pattern of values, attitudes, and responses. In this sense the study is a model of the procedures to be used in attempts to understand fully the agents and processes of socialization in any culture. However, although Bronfenbrenner draws comparisons between Soviet and American cultures, it is difficult to make any generalizations from these findings, interesting as they are. Valid cross-cultural generalizations about socialization require comparable data and multidimensional analyses of child-rearing practices and techniques of socialization in many cultures.

Pooling Data
from Many Cultures

Data from ethnographic studies of diverse cultures can be used to test the relationships between modal personality or behavioral properties and variables of family structure (complexity and distribution of authority) and functioning (decision-making, working as a unit). Such studies ". . . which collect data on a limited set of topics from many cultural units . . . [may be] advocated not as a substitute for the intensive ethnography of single people, but rather as a needed additional mode of data collection, particularly for those correlational types of analysis in which dozens of cultures are needed."[23]

Suppose it is hypothesized that participation in the family's economy and sustenance from a very early age induces strong tendencies to help others and to share possessions. The fact that in one culture children contribute substantially to the family's work and are also very helpful and generous to others outside the family is not by itself convincing evidence that the hypothesis is valid. The association between the variables may be explained in many possible ways, and few of them can be ruled out if we are looking at only one culture. But the hypothesis could be tested by examining data on the relevant variables (children's work and some assessments of generosity) from many cultures from different geographical areas. We could then determine whether, as the hypothesis predicts, helpfulness and generosity are more common among children from cultures with child labor than among those from cultures in which youngsters do not contribute to the family's economy.

The work of Harvard University's Beatrice and John Whiting and their colleagues[24] represents a notable step in the direction of systematic pooling of data from several cultures to determine the correlations between cultural variables and individuals' behavior. The aspect of their research that is of concern to us deals with children's altruism. The basic data consisted of naturalistic observations of 134 boys and girls between three and eleven years of age in six cultures, one each in Kenya, Mexico, the Phillippines, Okinawa, India, and a Yankee community in New England. Each child was observed for an average of seventeen five-minute periods, in a variety of social interactions—in courtyards near their homes, in the fields, on school grounds; with adults present or absent; during group work, play, or casual social activities. Every interaction was recorded and categorized into classes such as the following: shows symbolic aggression, offers help, reprimands, offers support, seeks dominance, seeks attention, suggests responsibly. These categories were reduced statistically by factor analysis to three major dimensions, one of which was *altruism versus egoistic behavior.* The behaviors most closely related to the altruistic extreme of this dimension were "offers help" (including food, toys, and helpful information), "offers support" and "suggests responsibly" (making helpful suggestions). The primary beneficiary of the interaction in each instance was another individual. In contrast, the behaviors loading most heavily on the egoistic end of the dimension ("seeks dominance," "seeks attention," and "seeks help") benefited the actor himself.

Most of the children in Kenyan, Mexican, and Phillippine cultures were high above the median of the total sample in altruism, while most of the children in the other three cultures (the Okinawan, Yankee, and Indian) scored low in altruism. The altruism-inducing cultures were then compared with the egoism-producing cultures on a number of sociocultural factors. In the altruistic cultures, the female role is an important one; women in these societies make major contributions to the economy and food supply. People in these cultures tend to live together in extended family groups. In contrast, in cultures where the independent, nuclear family units, consisting only of father, mother, and children, are more frequent, there are more egoistic children. In comparing complex with simpler societies, complex societies, those characterized by occupational specialization, a caste or class system, and centralized governments, were less conducive to the development of altruism. Apparently,

> in . . . simpler kin-oriented societies, with economies based upon subsistence gardening, altruistic behavior is highly valued and individual egoistic achievement frowned upon. Women must work in the fields, and the children must help in order for the family to subsist. To offer help, to support others, and to be responsible are taught both by precept and practice. Being helplessly dependent, showing off, boasting, and being egoistically dominant are incompatible with such a way of life.
>
> On the other hand, in the more complex societies, where no child knows what he is going to be when he grows up, individual achievement and success must be positively valued. To help a friend sitting next to you in an examination is defined as cheating. To ask for help from specialists such as mechanics,

dressmakers, shopkeepers, psychotherapists, priests, or servants
is expected and paid for in cash rather than in reciprocal
services.[25]

The cultural variable most closely associated with the altruism–egoism dimension was task assignment or taking on
responsibility (the extent to which children perform household tasks or chores related to the family's economic security).
As had been hypothesized by the investigators, "children
who . . . perform more domestic chores, help more with
economic tasks and spend more time caring for their infant
brothers, sisters, and cousins, score high on the altruistic vs.
egoistic dimension."[26]

Some of the findings of Bronfenbrenner's study in the
Soviet Union add further evidence supportive of this hypothesis.[27] One component of the Soviet school curriculum,
designed to instill a sense of social responsibility, is the early
assignment to children of responsibility for younger school-
mates whom they are expected to help with any problems,
particularly schoolwork. This assignment of responsibility to
Soviet children appears to achieve its objective; the children
develop a strong sense of consideration and responsibility
for others. This finding is consistent with the Whitings'
hypothesis.

It is a well-substantiated fact, based on considerable corroborative evidence, that cultural membership is a potent force
in shaping the child's personality characteristics, values, and
reactions, including responsiveness to others' needs, generosity,
helpfulness, and a sense of social responsibility. Anthropological and cross-cultural studies have seldom explored in
depth the question of *how* a culture instills these attributes or
responses. However, the recent work of a number of behav-

ioral scientists (the Whitings, Bronfenbrenner, Spiro) who specifically examine social structure and cultural practices antecedent to children's behavior yields some relevant information about the means by which the culture helps to socialize the child. Synthesizing the findings from many studies, we conclude that children are likely to develop high levels of prosocial behavior if they are raised in cultures characterized by (1) stress (from parents, peers, and other agents of socialization) on consideration of others, sharing, and orientation toward the group; (2) simple social organization or a traditional, rural setting; (3) assignment to women of important economic functions; (4) members of the extended family living together; and (5) early assignment of tasks and responsibility to children.

The most convincing, fine-grained data on the processes and mechanisms underlying socialization come from studies of child-rearing practices in the family, most of them conducted by Western researchers. We will proceed to discuss the findings of these studies shortly (see Chapter 6). However, before proceeding to that discussion, we will digress briefly to discuss some "person" variables, attributes of individuals (such as age, sex, social class, or personal qualities) that do not in themselves *determine* or shape responses but may be associated with strong or weak predispositions to prosocial behavior.

"Person" Variables and Prosocial Behavior

There are a number of characteristics of individuals that may be correlated with prosocial behavior but do not fit neatly into any of our major categories of *determinants*. We refer to variables such as sex, class membership, age, ordinal position, and some personal attributes. These cannot be considered *process* variables; they do not refer to actions or operations that in themselves govern prosocial responses or predispositions, nor can they directly promote or diminish these.

Rather, these characteristics may be functionally connected with *process* variables (mediating or intervening variables) that *do* influence or regulate prosocial behavior. To cite a simple example, the disciplinary practices parents use in rearing their daughters may differ considerably from those applied in rearing their sons. Therefore, if we discover that there are sex differences in prosocial predispositions, we may attribute these, at least in part, to the differential socialization (the mediating or intervening process) of the two sexes. Analogously, as we shall see, age is significantly correlated with level of sharing and helping. This correlation may simply reflect a link between age and two classes of determinants of prosocial behavior, socialization practices and cognitive processes. Perhaps parents of older children, compared with parents of younger ones, more frequently use techniques conducive to the development of helping and sharing. An alternative explanation rests on the fact that older children have attained higher levels of cognitive functioning and moral reasoning than younger ones have and this may account for the older children's higher levels of altruism. In this case cognitive maturity may be considered the variable mediating or intervening between age and prosocial responses. Finally, as many studies show, prosocial action may be associated with personal qualities that do not directly promote these actions but that are themselves the consequents of distinctive socialization experiences that also foster prosocial development. In brief, "person" or "participant" variables associated with prosocial responses are intimately linked with mediating variables that fall into one or more categories of determinants, such as socialization practices and cognitive determinants.

Age, sex, and social class sometimes act as "moderator variables," modifying the relationships between antecedents and prosocial actions. For example, sex would be a moderator variable if a cognitive measure, say role-taking ability, was found to be correlated with helping behavior in boys but not in girls. Analogously, age would be considered a moderator variable if identification with parents was correlated with helping or sharing among preschool children but not among seven-year-olds.

Social Class
and Prosocial Behavior

This is the simplest "person" variable to discuss because it has been repeatedly demonstrated that family socioeconomic status has no bearing on children's predispositions toward sharing or helping,[1] although, according to the findings of one study, middle-class children whose parents worked in bureaucratic settings were more helpful to others than their lower-class peers.[2] Adolescents and children from middle-class entrepreneurial families are more likely than peers from either other middle-class or lower-class families to consider reciprocity (helping someone who had previously helped them) a principal reason for offering help.[3]

Age

A fairly consistent pattern emerges from most investigations of the relationship between age and prosocial conduct. Nurturance of others, sharing, and helping are generally unrelated to age during the preschool period[4] but increase significantly with advancing age between four and thirteen.[5] This may be due to any of several factors or combinations of factors: the enrichment of role-taking and empathic abilities with greater maturity, age-related shifts in moral reasoning, increased skill in helping, or more frequently repeated exposures to inductive (reasoning) child-rearing techniques or parental affection.

Sex

On theoretical grounds, we might expect to find that boys and girls differ in prosocial activities, as they do in many personality and social characteristics. Nevertheless, the vast majority of investigators have failed to find any significant sex differences in prosocial orientations or responses.[6] There are only a few exceptions to this general conclusion. In some studies, girls have been found to be somewhat more helpful, generous, nurturant, and considerate than boys.[7] It is difficult to determine which of several alternative explanations of these sex differences in prosocial behavior is most reasonable. Girls apparently receive more affection from their mothers than boys do and are more likely to be disciplined by induction and less by power-oriented techniques. (See p. 94 for explanations of the consequences of use of these practices.) Or, as a result of their training, girls may be more empathic with the needs and distress of others.[8] Furthermore, in many cultures helpfulness and nurturance of others are considered more appropriate for girls than for boys; girls are therefore more frequently and more strongly rewarded for such behavior by parents and others.

Family Size
and Ordinal Position

No clear-cut or easily interpreted patterns of relationships between these factors and prosocial behavior have been discovered. Some investigators maintain that family size and sharing behavior are unrelated,[9] while others find that growing up in a large family promotes generosity.[10] According to the data of two other studies, small family size is related to helping in emergency situations.[11] The reasons for this last relationship are unclear, although the investigator speculates that children from small families may have a great deal of self-assurance and initiative and are consequently more willing to act spontaneously (without specific permission) to help another child.

Firstborn or older siblings in a family are more likely than middle or younger children to help a peer in distress and to share (or donate) generously.[12] According to naturalistic observations in six cultures, only children and the youngest children in a family tend to be more egoistic than others, seeking more help and attention but offering less help and support to peers.[13] These effects of ordinal position may be most parsimoniously interpreted in terms of social learning theory; older children are expected to help with their younger siblings and are frequently rewarded for being helpful and nurturant to them. These responses thus become strong and habitual; they are consequently generalized to interactions with others.

Personality Characteristics and Prosocial Behavior

As a result of a few landmark studies in social psychology and the psychology of personality, as well as a host of less prominent, supportive studies, it has become an accepted fact that certain forms of antisocial behavior are linked to specific personality traits and motives. Delinquency, violence, fascist and authoritarian orientations, and racial prejudice are associated with emotional insecurity, rigidity, suspiciousness, and hostility. To researchers in personality development, it seems intuitively reasonable to hypothesize that prosocial dispositions are also connected with personal characteristics and with deep-lying motives. However, a critical review of relevant empirical studies shows only partial support for this hypothesis. In many instances, the data yield no confirmation, and the findings of some studies contradict the results of others. In view of these facts, conclusions must be regarded as tentative and suggestive at best. A summary of the major findings follows.

Aggression, Activity Level, and Expressiveness

Young children who rank high in prosocial behavior tend to be active, outgoing, emotionally expressive, willing to seek help, and, according to several reports, moderately aggressive. Nursery school boys who were generous in sharing their winnings (candies) were independently rated by their teachers as significantly more outgoing, and gregarious, and less competitive, than stingy peers.[14] In other studies of nursery school children, expressiveness of feeling has been shown to be correlated with willingness to help a distressed character in a puppet show,[15] and overt displays of dependent needs correlated with nurturance of peers (helping and paying attention).[16] Apparently, children who have the freedom to express their own needs and feelings are more apt to assist others. In addition, kindergarten teachers considered boys in their class who tried to help a peer in distress more outgoing than those who did not help.[17]

The relationship between aggression and prosocial responses in nursery school children is a complex one. In a pioneering study, Murphy[18] found that two- to four-year-old children's sympathetic behavior was positively correlated with their aggressiveness, leadership, and resistance (teachers' ratings). These findings were replicated, for nursery school boys but not for girls, in a naturalistic study in which interpersonal aggression, both verbal and physical, was significantly correlated with nurturance (giving another child help, comfort, assurance, or affection).[19] Among three- to five-year-olds in another interesting study there was a more complex relationship between aggression and sharing, comforting and helping. Aggression and being the victim of aggression were positively correlated with sharing and comforting in boys relatively low in aggression (below the mean), but there was a *negative* association between overt aggression and prosocial behavior in the more aggressive boys (those above the mean in aggression).[20] Perhaps, as the investigators suggest, aggression that is manifested relatively infrequently is more an indication of assertiveness than of hostility and thus may be associated with greater likelihood of intervention to help others.

On the surface there seem to be some incongruities in these findings. On the one hand, those who are helpful and generous are more expressive of dependence and, on the other, they are more likely to manifest some aggression, although not high levels of hostile aggression. Perhaps assertiveness and the expression of dependence reflect emotional responsivity, activity, and outgoingness, qualities that may be prerequisite for the development of prosocial predispositions in the early years. Maybe "children who express their distress and/or who seek help are more easily affectively aroused and respond more to threats both to themselves and to others. . . . Perhaps the rendering of aid requires a quality of outgoingness, or a lack of interpersonal timidity, which is also often required of the child in expressing his distress or the seeking of help."[21]

Social and Emotional Adjustment

Strong predispositions to prosocial behavior in nursery and elementary school children are also associated with high ego strength, self-control, and good personal adjustment. Substantial support for this statement is derived from a broad-based, ongoing longitudinal study in which the personality characteristics of the nursery school participants were assessed by means of their teachers' Q-sort items. Those who were rated high in the characteristics "helpful and cooperative," "concerned with moral issues," and "considerate of other children" also scored high on an index of ego resiliency (ability to recover after stressful experiences) and low in tests of undercontrol (that is, they were *not* lacking in self-control). Adequate personal adjustment and ego strength at the age of four also predicted generosity (sharing and distributing rewards) at the age of five. Those who were generous at five had been described by their nursery school teachers a year earlier as bright, reasonable, generous, cooperative, considerate, planful, reflective, attentive, creative, dependable and responsible, calm, relaxed, and tending to recover readily after stressful experiences. In contrast, children low in generosity at the age of five were judged, at the age of four, as aggressive, unable to delay gratification, active, emotionally labile, restless and fidgety, afraid of being deprived, tending to overreact to frustrations, and behaving in immature and rattled ways after stress.[22]

The fourth-grade children participating in another study were deliberately overpaid for their work and then given a chance to donate some of their undeserved earnings to poor orphans. When donations were made anonymously, those capable of long delays of gratification, generally considered an index of ego strength or self-control, donated more than their peers who scored lower in delay of gratification.[23]

Other data suggest that there is a curvilinear relationship between amount of donation and measures of adjustment in fourth-grade boys who earned prizes and could donate some of their earnings to others. Compared with those who donated moderate amounts, the stingiest boys scored lower in personality tests of self-control, perseverance, and vigorousness, and the most generous showed more signs of maladjustment (emotional instability, proneness to guilt, and naivete). The best-adjusted boys apparently considered both their own and others' needs and made moderate donations. None of these relationships were found among the girls who participated in the study.[24]

Among preadolescents, the most altruistic (assessed by peer nominations) scored higher than their less altruistic peers in self-report tests of ego strength and self-esteem. The altruists were more self-confident, more satisfied with peer relation-ships, and more self-assured.[25] Findings reinforcing these come from other studies of children of several age groups that demonstrated that helping, consideration, and donating are related to personal competence, initiative in social inter-actions,[26] and measures of social responsibility.[27] All these variables reflect self-confidence and ego strength. Similar results were found in studies of adults.[28]

Overall, the data derived from a variety of studies, using diverse research methods and involving participants of many age levels, are highly consistent and hence permit some ten-tative conclusions about the correlations between personality structure and prosocial behavior. Compared with their peers, children with strong prosocial dispositions appear to be better adjusted, more socially responsible, more expressive, and more active in many ways, being gregarious and somewhat aggres-sive.

The relationships discovered are somewhat fragile, how-ever. Some of them have been replicated and some have not. This is unfortunate, for the discovery of clear-cut and direct connections between personality characteristics and prosocial behavior would have many theoretical and practical impli-cations. Assume, for a moment, that self-esteem in children is closely associated with helping behavior. Then, we might infer that high self-esteem and strong predispositions to altruism are both consequents of the same family socialization experiences. *If* the socialization antecedents of self-esteem were well understood, and *if* this knowledge could be applied successfully in raising children's self-esteem, increases in children's tendencies to help others would automatically follow. But this would occur *only* if the correlations between self-esteem and prosocial conduct were high and replicated in a number of studies. In fact, these conditions do not obtain. There are very few relationships between children's personality traits and prosocial dispositions that are substantial, well-established, and reliable. In brief, we cannot make valid inferences about the family socialization practices that shape prosocial conduct from correlations between altruism or sharing and personality characteristics. The impacts of child-rearing techniques on children's dispositions toward prosocial action must be studied directly. Indeed, this has been the central topic of some important research projects, and we turn our attention to these in the next chapter.

CHAPTER

6

Socialization
in the Family

Cultures are remarkably successful in inculcating in their members approved patterns of behavior, values, norms, personal characteristics, and behavioral predispositions. These qualities and behaviors are generally adaptive, enabling members of the group to satisfy their own needs, relate to each other, and at the same time maintain the continuity and functioning of the society itself. Moreover, since they are "normal" or standard in the group, these traits or responses are manifested frequently and relatively consistently in diverse situations. What is standard may vary greatly from group to group. Mexican-American children in the Southwest, Hopi children on the reservations, and youngsters in Israeli kibbutzim are usually kind, considerate, and cooperative; Ik children, in contrast, are rarely generous, kindhearted, or considerate.

Yet the cultures in which children are reared do not completely control their propensities to behave prosocially. In practically every culture there is considerable variability in characteristics such as cooperativeness and generosity among members. In complex societies such as our own, the spectrum includes saints and consistently self-sacrificing Good Samaritans as well as unmitigated Scrooges—and there are many at every point in between.

To understand the development of these individual differences in prosocial behavior and orientations, we must turn our attention to the detailed study of variations in socialization practices *within* cultures. This means examining precisely what the chief agents of socialization (especially parents, but also peers, teachers, religious authorities, the mass media) actually *do* to enhance or restrict the development of prosocial behavior. Family members, particularly parents, are ordinarily the earliest and most significant agents of socialization. It is therefore to be expected that they will make the greatest contribution to the child's socialization, and that the personal characteristics and behavioral predispositions acquired in the family setting will be enduring and resistant to change.

Every child-rearing practice and technique of discipline may potentially affect children's behavior: demonstration or modeling (performing behaviors that may be emulated); nurturance (caring for the child with warmth, support, and affection); praise and approval; giving or withholding love or material rewards; explanation and example of rules; lecturing, and giving "lessons"; corporal and psychological punishment. All of these, and many others, are used by parents in the process of socialization.

The impacts of many kinds of practices and parent–child relationships on prosocial behavior have been examined in depth, as we shall see. But no investigation can be concerned with all of them. Consequently, each study typically centers on one, or a few, critical variable(s), selected largely on the basis of the investigator's theoretical orientation. One investigator may conduct research on parental nurturance as a major antecedent variable or regulator of children's prosocial responses, while another, approaching the problem from a different theoretical perspective, will focus on the consequences of using reasoning in discipline. After the antecedent variables to be investigated have been defined, appropriate and objective methods of assessing them must be devised. There are no standardized or adequately validated procedures for measuring socialization practices, and each can be assessed in diverse ways. For example, parental nurturance can be evaluated by means of intensive observations in the home; by interviewing parents or children or both, or by having them respond to questionnaires about child-training; by observing parents and children in a "situational test," a contrived but lifelike setting in which a parent and child interact; or by administering Q-sorts to parents or children or both. (A child-rearing Q-sort technique is a form of rating procedure in which the rater—for instance, the mother—is given a set of adjectives or statements such as "I believe in letting my child make decisions about most things" and "I let my child know when I feel angry," and sorts them into seven piles according to the degree to which they are accurate or descriptive. Those that really "hit home" are placed in pile 7 and those that are not at all applicable in pile 1.)[1]

Each of these assessment techniques has proven useful in studies of parent–child relationships and their effects on the development of prosocial behavior. The present chapter is devoted primarily to studies of this kind. However, a number of interesting experimental or laboratory investigations concentrate on experimental analogues (models or representa-

tions) of parent–child interactions. In these studies socialization practices and family interactions are reproduced
in miniature form; aspects of these interactions are then varied and changes in the child's behavior are assessed. Suppose,
for instance, that an investigator hypothesizes that parental
modeling of prosocial behavior (performing prosocial acts
that are observed by the child) strengthens children's propensities toward such behavior. In an experimental test of this
hypothesis, children observe an adult model (presumably
representing a mother or father) playing a game and winning
prizes. Some participants also watch the model as she shares
these prizes with a child; others, a control group, observe the
model playing the game but not sharing the winnings. After-
wards the children themselves play the game, collect prizes,
and then have an opportunity to share their winnings. If the
children who observed the model's sharing share their prizes
with others while the controls do not, we might conclude,
correctly, that adult modeling of sharing increases children's
tendencies to share. Such an experiment provides valuable
information about imitation as a fundamental process in the
development of sharing behavior. But further tests would be
necessary to determine whether this prosocial behavior is
temporary or lasting, specific to the particular situation or
generalized.

Can we generalize from the findings of experiments to the
probable consequences of certain socialization practices in the
family? That is, are the experimental situations really
accurate representations of what occurs in the home? If children in a laboratory imitate a model's performance, can we
conclude that they will ordinarily copy a parent's behavior at
home? If manipulations of an experimental situation alter
prosocial responses in discernible ways, it seems entirely reasonable to infer that many repetitions of comparable events in

the real world would have similar—and perhaps more pronounced and more lasting—consequences. Yet we cannot be
certain that such inferences are valid without testing them
directly in family settings.

As we see it, the experimental studies are extremely useful in
clarifying the fundamental mechanisms underlying socialization, including the acquisition of prosocial responses. But the
experiments are not, strictly speaking, investigations of socialization, because the contrived situations are radically different from those the child encounters at home. In an experiment, the child usually observes the model's performance only
once, or at most a few times. In addition, the model is in most
cases a stranger to the child. Real life models are frequently
parents with whom the child identifies and there is a long
history of continuous, close, and usually affectionate, model–
child interactions. For these reasons we must be very cautious about generalizing from experimental operations to
the course of socialization in the family. We shall review a few
of the most pertinent laboratory studies in this chapter.

Because there are numerous correlational studies of child-
rearing antecedents of children's prosocial tendencies that
have used diverse research methods, it is difficult to integrate
the accumulated findings. Nevertheless, some substantial,
practical conclusions can be drawn; these will be presented in
this chapter. For the convenience of discussion, the rest of the
chapter is organized according to the antecedent variables
investigated, beginning with modeling and identification, a
process that resembles imitation in many ways. We regard
these as the most powerful socialization antecedents of prosocial predispositions. The effects of modeling are augmented if
the model is also nurturant (helping, kindly, affectionate, encouraging); we shall also discuss research on this issue. In a
later section of the chapter, we shall examine the conse-

quences of nurturance per se on the development of prosocial behavior (see pp. 90–92).

Modeling and Identification

Experimental Studies of Modeling

In the typical modeling experiment, some children observe a model performing prosocial acts, for example, donating prizes he or she has won (pennies, candies, or coupons that can be redeemed for toys) to needy children. A control group does not observe the prosocial behavior. Subsequently, each child has an opportunity to donate something that he or she has won to charity. The effects of modeling are ascertained by comparing the donations of the children in the experimental and control groups.

One of the findings of experimental studies of modeling prosocial behavior has been replicated many times: the observation of a model performing prosocial acts is likely to elevate the levels of children's generosity, helping, and sharing substantially, at least temporarily, and often for long periods. The effects of a model's selfish behavior have not been so clearly delineated. Some, but not all, investigators have found that after children observe a selfish or stingy model, they reduce their own donations.[2]

Studies of the durability and generalizability of the effects of prosocial modeling have yielded some highly provocative results. For example, the six- to ten-year-old participants in one study observed a model donating liberally and were able to rehearse generous behavior voluntarily. The positive effects of this modeling lasted for seven days and, in addition, the generalization of imitative donations was apparent in another, quite different situation three weeks later.[3] Data from the studies show that watching a model's generosity had effects that were still detectable two to four months later.[4] Moreover, children who imitated a model's liberal donations of candy were also more generous than controls in sharing pennies with peers.[5] Children's donations of chips, each worth a penny anonymously, after observing a generous model (without anyone knowing about it) was generalized to donations of candy in a classroom setting ten days later.[6] Months after observing a model playing a game and making generous donations from his winnings, children between seven and eleven years of age played the same game, in a different room, with another experimenter and with a different potential beneficiary of their donations. Nevertheless, they donated significantly greater amounts than controls, thus demonstrating significant generalization—over time and across situations—of prosocial behavior.[7]

After a thorough survey of the literature on modeling, Rushton reached a strong positive conclusion: ". . . It would appear that relatively brief exposure to highly salient models *can* produce durable and generalizable behavior change in observers. Thus there is reason to believe that modeling studies *are* analogous to the processes that occur in the natural environment."[8]

Effects of the Model's Power and Nurturance.   Not all models are equally successful in inducing imitation of prosocial behavior. What kinds of models, or what aspects of a model's behavior, evoke imitation? It has been hypothesized that powerful and nurturant (warm and interested) models are most effective, and the consequences of power and nurturance have been explored separately in many studies. Model's power, the less frequently studied variable, is defined as control of resources, the capability of administering rewards and punishments to the child. In general, research findings indicate that powerful models evoke more imitation than those without power. For example, in one study, the model was powerful because he was in a position to select a child for a special prize. Children between seven and eleven years of age emulated this model's sharing behavior more frequently than they imitated a weaker model's sharing.[9] However, in at least one study, labeling the model as powerful (for example, a future teacher at the school) failed to raise children's tendencies to imitate his helping behavior.[10] It appears that models are more apt to be effective in evoking imitation of helping and generosity if they are in direct control, as agents of reinforcements.[11]

More investigations have been concerned with the impact of the model's nurturance on his or her ability to elicit imitation, and here, too, the results are equivocal. The relevant experiments usually start with a brief interaction (ten to fifteen minutes) between the child and a model. The model is nurturant (warm, friendly, kindly, and responsive) to some of the children, but aloof and indifferent (nonnurturant) with another group. The children are then exposed to the model performing some prosocial act, and, subsequently, the child has a chance to imitate that behavior. Nurturance preceding exposure to the model's sharing appears to have no effect on the altruism or charitability of elementary school children or may actually diminish them.[12] But nurturance by the model preceding her modeling of helping—specifically, aiding a peer whose cries of distress are heard—heightens children's tendencies to imitate these actions.[13] It has been suggested that the differential effects of the model's nurturance on children's donating and helping are attributable to the fact that nurturance communicates to the child that "he may do what he wishes: in the case of the donation to not donate; in the case of rescue activity to reduce his empathically produced distress by relieving the distress of another."[14] The model's nurturance may also indicate that the adult is not likely to punish the child for initiating helping behavior. "This interpretation seems plausible in the light of research findings . . . which suggest that children fear disapproval for initiating action that is not clearly permissible."[15] We can draw only limited conclusions from these experimental studies in which the nurturant interactions were few (often only one) and of a brief duration. But more frequent and consistent nurturance, extended over a longer period, may have more pronounced and unequivocal effects on the model's effectiveness. This was clearly demonstrated in an outstanding experimental study by Yarrow, Scott, and Waxler[16] that, in our opinion, duplicated the family situation more adequately than any of the other experiments we have reviewed.

Before the actual modeling sessions in this study began, the children's original propensities for helping were measured. This was accomplished by observing their reactions to pictures of people or animals in distress (for example, a picture of a child falling off a bike and getting hurt) and to four actual behavioral instances of distress, such as a kitten tangled in yarn struggling toward its mother.

The caretaker (who later served as the model) spent a great deal of time establishing herself as a meaningful adult in the child's life. Specifically, she took care of the children, preschoolers between three and one-half and five and one-half years of age, and worked with them a half-hour a day for five days spaced over two weeks. With half of them, she was consistently nurturant, initiating friendly interactions, offering help and support freely, sympathizing and protecting, expressing confidence in the children's abilities, and praising them frequently. With the other half of the participants she was consistently nonnurturant, aloof, ignoring their requests, detached, and only minimally helpful.

After these two weeks of child–model interactions, the modeling sessions were begun. Each child participated in two modeling sessions, separated by two days, in which she or he worked individually with the model. Some of the children who had experienced high nurturance from the model and some who had encountered low nurturance observed the model being altruistic in dioramas (miniature reproductions) of distress situations involving children, families, or animals. There were duplicates of each diorama set; the model had one and the child had the other. The adult's modeling always included her

> (a) verbalized awareness of the distress, (b) her sympathy and help for the victim, (c) her pleasure or relief at the comfort or well-being that resulted, and (d) her use of the word "help" to summarize what had been done. For example, she turned to the first diorama, the monkey trying to reach the banana, and said, "Oh, Mr. Monkey, you must be hungry. You can't reach your food. I'll help you. Here's your banana. Now you won't be hungry." She then uncovered the paired diorama and told the child that it was his turn. If the child retrieved the banana for the monkey, the adult said, "I think the monkey feels better because you gave him his food. He isn't hungry now." If the child did not help, the adult went on to the next set of dioramas, repeating the procedures.[17]

A second group, consisting of some children who had been highly nurtured and some who had low nurturance by the model, observed another kind of modeling. In their training sessions the model exhibited altruism with the dioramas and, in addition, showed concern and aided another individual under realistic distress conditions. For example, at one point during a training session, another adult came into the room, tried to retrieve some of the children's supplies, and banged her head against the table. She winced and held her head. The

model responded warmly, putting her hand on the confederate's shoulder and saying, "I hope you aren't hurt.
Do you want to sit down a minute?" The victim responded
appreciatively.

Two days after the last training session, the altruistic responses of the children were tested again with a new series of
pictures and dioramas and two behavioral incidents. Then,
two weeks later, there was an additional session to evaluate the
durability and generalization of the effects of training. In this
session, the children were taken individually to a neighboring
house to visit a mother and her baby, and, while there, they
could help the mother by picking up a basket of spools or
buttons that had spilled or by retrieving toys the baby had
dropped out of her crib.

The two types of modeling were found to have vastly different effects on children's prosocial behavior. Modeling of
helpfulness with dioramas only, unrelated to actual experiences with other people, produced less increment in altruistic
responses than modeling with dioramas *and* helping in "live"
interactions. On the tests given two days after the end of the
training, those trained exclusively with dioramas showed increases only in symbolic altruism, that is, in diorama situations; their altruism was not generalized to pictured situations
or to real life incidents. Exposure to a model actually helping
other people was much more effective in promoting children's
helping behavior, especially if the model was nurturant. On
the follow-up test two weeks after the training, those who had
been exposed to extended modeling from a nurturant adult
were more likely to express sympathy and to help the mother
or baby in the home setting than children in any other group.
Eighty-four percent of these children spontaneously gave help
in these situations, although only 24 percent of them had
helped in the original, pretraining behavioral incidents. The

authors therefore concluded that "the optimal condition for the development of sympathetic helpful behavior was one in which children observed an adult manifesting altruism at every level—in principle and in practice, both toward the child and toward others in distress."[18] "Only when extensive training was conducted in the context of the developed, nurturant interaction was altruistic behavior significantly increased."[19]

Extrapolating from the results of their study, the investigators make some practical suggestions about socialization by parents:

> The parent who conveys his values to the child didactically as tidy principles, and no more, accomplishes only that learning in the child. Generalized altruism would appear to be best learned from parents who do not only try to inculcate the principles of altruism, but who also manifest altruism in everyday interactions. Moreover, their practices toward their children are consistent with their general altruism.
>
> Emphasis on the role of nurturance in the rearing environment does not suggest that it is sufficient. The data demonstrate its importance along with the specific modeling, accompanied by the model's verbal communications. The model communicated a good deal about her altruism by identifying the cues to which she was reacting, the inferences she was making about the victims, and her affect in aiding them. She also supplied a bridging label of "help" which was common to each of the events. The cognitive aspects of the training, the labels for her behavior, it is assumed, were probably significant aids to the child's acquiring and generalizing helping.[20]

Parental Modeling and Generosity

Correlation studies substantiate the findings of this experimental study in demonstrating that repeated adult modeling, particularly when it is combined with nurturance from the model, may have powerful and generalized beneficial effects. In a study of generosity among nursery school boys, the subjects played a game, won some candies, and then had an opportunity to share their winnings with friends. The criterion of generosity was the amount they were willing to share, and this measure was significantly correlated with independent ratings of generosity by the nursery school teachers.[21] Those who shared most and those who shared least were given a projective, semi-structured doll play situation in which they expressed their views of their parents, of themselves, and of their interactions with their parents. Compared with the others, the most generous boys much more frequently portrayed their fathers as nurturant and warm parents and as models of generosity, sympathy, and compassion. It appears that parental modeling and nurturance, like modeling and nurturance in experimental settings, are powerful antecedents of sharing. It may be inferred that the father's warmth and nurturance produced strong identification with him and, consequently, imitation of his patterns of generosity and sympathy. Unfortunately, there were no assessments of the fathers' actual behavior, so it is impossible to tell whether the generous boys' fathers were, in fact, more highly nurturant and generous. In any case, it is clear that the generous boys perceived their fathers as having these characteristics.

Parental Modeling and Consideration

Hoffman assessed fifth-grade pupils' reputations for altruism and consideration of others, by means of sociometric questionnaires.[22] Children nominated the three same-sexed classmates who were *most* likely to "care about how other kids feel and try not to hurt their feelings" and "to stick up for some kid that the other kids are making fun of or calling names." At the same time, their parents were asked to rank eighteen values in order of importance in their own value systems. These included values like "showing consideration of others' feelings," "putting work before play," "going out of one's way to help other people." Presumably parents who placed high values on altruism will provide good models of caring, helping, and consideration.

The fathers of the most helpful and considerate boys, and the mothers of the girls with these characteristics ranked altruism high in their own hierarchy of values. Apparently, the level of altruism of the parent of the same sex has the most impact on the child's propensity to perform altruistic acts. This is undoubtedly related to the fact that, at this age, children are likely to identify most strongly with the parent of their own sex and, consequently, to incorporate and imitate that parent's behavior, attitudes, and motives.

Studies of Adult Altruists

A number of fascinating investigations of the developmental histories of unusual prosocial adults are highly relevant to the present discussion. The research techniques used in these studies, primarily interviews and questionnaires, were far different from those used in the studies of children. Yet the results were in many ways comparable, and the findings have distinct and significant developmental implications. They provide further evidence of the influences of parental modeling and nurturance on later altruism and predispositions to prosocial behavior.

Christians Who Saved Jews from the Nazis. One dramatic study, primarily the work of Perry London of the University of Southern California and David Rosenhan of

Stanford University, was focused on twenty-seven Christians who during World War II risked their lives in efforts to rescue Jews from the Nazis. Because of lack of funds the study was never completed, but pilot work gave the researchers some definite impressions about the characteristics that predisposed these people to such humane, altruistic acts. Three qualities were predominant: a spirit of adventurousness; a sense of being socially marginal; and, most relevant for our purposes, intense identification with a parental model, not necessarily of the same sex, who was a model of moral orientation and conduct. Some of the parents were religious moralists, others were ideological moralists. In any case, having a moralistic parent serving as a model for identification was a powerful determinant of later self-sacrifice and altruism.[23]

A Study of Freedom Riders.   The findings of the study of the rescuers reviewed above, although tentative and pre-liminary, led Rosenhan[24] to another highly relevant study, a study of Freedom Riders, workers who were active in the Civil Rights Movement of the late 1950s and 1960s. These young adults participated in marches, sometimes for hun-dreds of miles, protested, picketed, and gave speeches in behalf of equal rights and opportunities for blacks. These activities entailed tremendous expenditures of effort and energy as well as considerable self-sacrifice of money and comfort; in addition, they were carried out at the cost of encountering a great deal of hostility and even physical assault from opposing forces. Some civil rights workers were murdered, and many were cruelly insulted, humiliated, and beaten.

Rosenhan differentiated two types of Freedom Riders. The first type, the *fully committed,* guided by what the investigator labeled internalized or autonomous altruism, were active for a year or longer, often giving up their homes, occupations, and educations to engage in the civil rights movement. The second type, the *partially committed,* limited their activities to one or two freedom rides or marches without much sacrifice of other pursuits, basic comforts, or their way of life. The two groups did *not* differ in attitudes; they were equally strong believers in the equality of whites and blacks.

What then accounts for the differences in their level of activism or active altruism, in their willingness and ability to devote time and energy to this work and to sacrifice for the welfare of others? Extensive interviews with the participants indicated that modeling, identification, and nurturance were of central importance. The parents of the fully committed were excellent models of prosocial behavior and concern with the welfare of others. When the fully committed Freedom Riders were children, their parents had vigorously worked for altruistic causes, and had protested against Nazi atrocities, religious restrictions, and other injustices. Thus, as children, the fully committed Freedom Riders had witnessed their parents' commitment and efforts and had shared their emotions. By contrast, the parents of the partially committed were "at best, mere verbal supporters of prosocial morality and at worst, critical about those moralities. It was common for our partially committed to report that their parents preached one thing and practiced another."[25] These parents provided symbolic but not behavioral modeling of prosocial behavior, and, as a result, their children became only partially committed, less thoroughly altruistic, than the others.

In addition, and consonant with the results of the experimental studies reviewed above, parental nurturance reinforced the effects of modeling, especially in the case of the fully committed. Specifically, the fully committed asserted that they had always had warm, respecting, and loving relationships with their parents during childhood and continuing through early adulthood, the time at which they became

Freedom Riders. These interactions with their parents undoubtedly promoted identification and, consequently, the
adoption of parental standards, values, and patterns of behavior. In contrast, the partially committed frequently described their relationships with their parents as avoidant,
cool, negative, or ambivalent; many reported that their chief
reactions to their parents were discomfort, anxiety, hostility,
and guilt.

Strong predispositions to prosocial actions in adulthood,
manifested in altruism and deep commitments to justice and
equality—and willingness to devote substantial time and energy to work for these—appear to have the same antecedents as
different forms of prosocial behavior, such as helping and
sharing, in childhood. Adult prosocial actions are, in part, the
consequents of observation of strong and consistent models
(usually parents) who show their own profound prosocial attitudes in both word and deed, and who, in addition, are
nurturant and loving, thus strengthening their children's
tendency to identify with and imitate the model (parent).

Parental Nurturance

Since parental nurturance often amplifies the prosocial
effects of direct modeling and identification, it does not seem
unreasonable to hypothesize that such nurturance by itself
might foster increased consideration of others, helpfulness,
and generosity. Parental nurturance may be regarded as a
kind of modeling of prosocial behavior; by being nurturant,
parents model consideration, kindness, and sympathy.

Available data offer only limited support for this hypothesis, however. While some investigators have found that parental nurturance stimulates the development of generosity,[26]
others fail to confirm this. Thus, the nursery school partici-

pants in the study imitated a nurturant model-caretaker's kindness and affection toward toy animals, while a group of peers duplicated a nonnurturant caretaker's aggressive and aloof behavior. The caretaker's nurturance had no generalized effect on the child's nurturance or aggression in their interactions with other children, however.[27]

Parental nurturance and affection have significant positive effects on preadolescents' consideration of others. Seventh-grade pupils' reputations for consideration of others were assessed by nominations from classmates. Their views of their parents' treatment of them were evaluated by means of report forms administered to lower- and middle-class children. (Middle-class parents were given similar report forms to fill out.) These forms listed eight possible reactions to the child's "doing something good" (giving affection, approval, qualified approval, material reward) and respondents indicated along the four point scale how often the parents reacted in these ways.

Among the middle-class boys and girls, consideration for others was found to be directly related to the mother's affection but not to the father's. Among the lower class, both maternal and paternal affection were related to boys' but not to girls' consideration of others. In general, then, these findings are consistent with the hypothesis that nurturance, particularly maternal nurturance, fosters the development of prosocial behavior. For unknown reasons, the relationship does not obtain in the case of lower-class girls.[28]

Other relevant studies have yielded even more equivocal results. In one of Feshbach's studies,[29] the generosity of middle class six- and eight-year-olds was assessed by two different tests; in one, being generous meant giving up playing with a valuable toy, and, in the other, it meant sharing candies with a peer. Q-sorts completed by the children's mothers and fathers supplied the basic data for evaluating parental socialization practices. Generosity in boys was found to be significantly correlated with paternal affection and with maternal child-centeredness and affectionate acceptance of the child, and negatively correlated with paternal rejection and dissatisfaction with the child. However, these relationships between parental nurturance and generosity did not hold in the case of girls.

Hoffman used reputation among peers (peer nominations on sociometric questionnaires) as the criterion of the consideration and helpfulness of preadolescents.[30] Some of his findings partially confirmed Feshbach findings, but others were contradictory. Specifically, maternal affection toward sons (inferred from the mothers' own reports) was positively associated with the boys' standing on these prosocial attributes. However, maternal affection was not related to girls' consideration and paternal affection was not significantly associated with either the boys' or girls' prosocial tendencies.

Given the evidence, we cannot draw any definitive conclusions about the impact of parental nurturance per se on children's prosocial behavior. Perhaps the simplest and most straightforward conclusion is that simply giving a child warmth, support, and affection (even in fairly large doses) does not ensure that the child will become altruistic, kind, considerate, or generous. Nurturance is most effective in strengthening predispositions toward prosocial behavior when it is part of a pattern of child-rearing that prominently features the modeling of prosocial acts.

Disciplinary Techniques: Power Assertion and Induction

The ways parents discipline their children are likely to affect their children's attitudes toward themselves and toward others. These orientations, in turn, may be expected to help mold children's prosocial inclinations and behavior. For example, in disciplining a child, the parent effectively models certain kinds of behavior. A parent who uses physical force or threat is acting as an aggressive model and, at the same time, shows the child aggression achieves some goals. If parents reason with their children, pointing out the "rights" and "wrongs" of their actions, they inevitably model consideration for others, and, at the same time, stress the social implications of one's own behavior, thus strengthening their children's empathic tendencies.

Empirical data offer at least partial support for these speculations. Parental disciplinary techniques do, in fact, have an appreciable effect on children's behavior. Some techniques appear to intensify children's predispositions toward prosocial behavior, while others tend to deter their development.

Extensive pioneering research on these issues has been conducted by Martin Hoffman of the University of Michigan and his colleagues.[31] In one of their most influential studies, a study of seventh-grade pupils in Detroit, attention was centered on consideration of others, the degree of consideration being operationally defined, as in some other studies of Hoffman's (see pp. 86–87), by the number of peer nominations for the positions of the classmate "most likely to care about other children's feelings" and "most likely to defend a child being made fun of by the group." Data on parental discipline were obtained by asking parents to imagine four situations (for example, the child delaying complying with a parental request to do something, or the child being careless and destroying something of value that belonged to another child). Parents designated their three most likely reactions to each situation, choosing these reactions from a list of fourteen possibilities (for example, thanking the child, explaining how the other child would feel about the destruction of a toy). The disciplinary practices listed fell into three main categories or types. The first, *power assertion,* refers to control by physical power or material resources, exemplified by physical punishment, deprivation of material objects or privileges, force, or the threat of these. *Love withdrawal,* the second type of discipline investigated, includes ignoring or isolating the child, refusing to speak to him or her. The third technique, *induction,* consists of reasoning with the child, explaining the painful consequences of the child's act for himself, for others, or for the parent. Examples of this are telling the child that his or her actions hurt the parent, saying the object damaged was highly valued by the parent, or referring to concern for another child.

For girls, the frequent use of power assertion by the mother was associated with *low* levels of consideration for others, while the use of induction was positively associated with a reputation for being considerate. The use of *love withdrawal* techniques, though, was not consistently related to this form of prosocial behavior. In brief, a pattern of infrequent power assertion and frequent induction by middle-class mothers generally facilitates the development of girls' prosocial behavior.

The findings for boys were quite different and unexpected: the consideration of others was positively related to parental use of power assertive techniques and unrelated to induction. The investigators suggest that the measure of consideration may not have been an adequate one for boys. "In particular there is no built-in provision to assume that the behavior is based on internal motivation. The motive behind such behavior in the case of boys might instead often be a need for approval by peers.... Consideration [of others] is a more deviant value for boys than girls."[32]

The investigators concluded that the use of induction techniques is conducive to the development of prosocial behavior. This is largely attributable, they believe, to the fact that induction is "most capable of eliciting the child's natural proclivities for empathy."[33] Power assertive techniques, on the other hand, are least effective in stimulating the development of consideration for others. In using this technique, the parent communicates that external power and authority, rather than appraisal of the consequences of one's actions for others, are the appropriate bases for deciding what action to take. In addition, the use of power assertion is not conducive to the

> internalization of control because it elicits intense hostility in the child and simultaneously provides him with a model for expressing that hostility outward. . . . Furthermore, [power assertion] makes the child's need for love less salient and functions as an obstacle to the arousal of empathy. Finally, it sensitizes the child to the punitive responses of adult authorities, thus contributing to an externally focussed moral orientation.[34]

These conclusions about the powerful influences of induction on prosocial behavior have also been substantiated by results of other studies that employed different criteria of prosocial behavior and participants of different ages. For example, in an earlier study, Hoffman[35] observed preschool children's helping behavior and sensitivity toward others, and also measured maternal socialization techniques by interviewing the mothers in detail about their interactions with their children on the previous day, presumably a typical one. Frequent use of induction by mothers, accompanied by low frequency of power assertion, was found to be a significant antecedent of high levels of preschoolers' sensitivity to others' needs and direct helpfulness to peers.

The participants in another study were fifth- and eighth-grade students at a Catholic school. They answered questionnaires about their perceptions of maternal disciplinary techniques, nominated the boys and girls in their classes who were kindest and most considerate, and were given opportunities to donate money to a charitable organization (UNICEF). In addition, the children responded to a self-report scale on values, ranking in order of personal importance twelve statements, such as "having a beautiful home and car" and "getting a job that helps other people." These rankings were the source of scores on self-centered values (material possessions, self-importance) and other-centered values (concern for others).

Maternal use of inductive techniques was found to be a good predictor of children's prosocial tendencies. At each age level studied, boys and girls who reported that their mothers frequently used induction in discipline were regarded as more considerate by their classmates, attached greater importance to other-centered values, and donated more of their earnings to charity. In contrast, the use of power assertion by the mother was associated with predominantly self-centered values and stinginess in donations.[36]

The generalized effects of induction techniques and the opposite effects of power assertive techniques are also apparent in the study of six- to eight-year-old boys' willingness to share candies with a peer and willingness to give up playing with a desirable toy so that another peer could use the toy. Parents' responses to Q-sort questionnaires provided information about a variety of child-rearing practices, such as induction and positive reinforcement, parental child-centeredness, affection, acceptance, and paternal emphasis on affection and autonomy. Maternal use of induction was found to be related to generosity in boys, and power assertive techniques (authoritarianism, restrictiveness, criticism, rejection of the child) tended to reduce generosity.[37]

Another kind of disciplinary induction technique that parents often use involves *reparation*, that is, calling the child's attention to the harm that has been done and encouraging him or her to consider the victim's feelings and to make reparations or to apologize or both. In a study of fifth-grade children, the frequent use of reparation-centered discipline by the opposite sex parent was found to be a powerful predictor of children's reputations for considerateness and helpfulness (classmates' nominations): the mothers' use of this technique was significantly correlated with boys' considerateness ($r = .50, p = .01$), while the fathers' use of it was associated with prosocial tendencies among the girls ($r = .53, p = .01$).[38]

There is a high degree of consistency in the findings from these varied studies, and all of them lead to the same conclusions: The frequent use of power assertive techniques (and parental attitudes reflecting these techniques) tends to diminish the level of children's prosocial behavior, while the extensive use of induction techniques facilitates the development of prosocial orientations.

Maturity Demands and Assignments of Responsibility

By reasoning with their children, parents demonstrate their respect for them and, at the same time, make it explicit that they hold high standards for the child. In a thorough, in-depth study, Diana Baumrind, a psychologist at the Institute of Human Development of the University of California, examined the effects of what she called *muturity demands,* specifically, parental maintenance of high standards, together with control and pressures on children to behave in mature ways, that is, to achieve in accordance with their abilities, and to assume responsibilities consistent with their levels of maturity. High maturity demands proved to be a significant antecedent of nursery school children's manifestations of social responsibility, specifically, their altruism and nurturance toward others, assessed by means of intensive, naturalistic observations by trained observers.[39]

Children gain in prosocial behavior if they are encouraged to assume responsibility for others. This result is entirely congruent with the finding that children reared in cultures in which there is considerable early assignment of responsibility are more helpful and supportive of peers than children in cultures that do not stress early assumption of responsibility for others.[40]

Recall, also, that in the Soviet Union, part of the elementary school curriculum consists of taking responsibility for assisting younger children with their school work and with their problems. The purpose of this assignment is the enhancement of predispositions toward helping and sharing among the pupils. The data from the studies reviewed here suggest that this goal is likely to be achieved by this means (see p. 62).

There is, in addition, some interesting experimental support for the hypothesis that taking on responsibilities is likely to raise the levels of children's prosocial proclivities. Some of the children participating in one study were taught to make puzzles so that they could later teach younger children to construct similar puzzles to be donated to hospitalized children. Other children, the controls, also learned to make these puzzles so that they themselves could later make more to give to hospitalized children, but were not assigned any responsibility for teaching others. A few days after they had learned how to make puzzles, all the subjects received gift certificates and were then asked to donate some of these to needy children. Some weeks later the children were asked to do some work that would benefit poor orphans, and still later, they were asked how many puzzles they would make for hospitalized children. Responsibility for teaching other children had

significant effects on at least some, but not all, of these prosocial activities; children of both sexes who had been assigned
such responsibility donated more gift certificates and made
more puzzles for hospitalized children than the children in the
control group.[41]

On balance, the results are fairly consistent, and it may
therefore be inferred that empirical evidence is supportive of
the hypothesis that assuming responsibility (including the
responsibility for teaching others) has a positive effect on
prosocial behavior. The effects may be limited, however, and
little is known of their durability.

The evidence from almost all relevant studies supports the
proposition that dispositions to prosocial behavior have their
roots in the home situation, specifically in parent–child relationships. Information on child-rearing practices has been
derived from diverse sources, different criteria of prosocial
behavior have been used, and the participants in the studies
vary widely in age. Yet, the consistency of the findings of the
studies, the degree to which they corroborate each other, is
impressive.

A number of substantial conclusions can be drawn:
Modeling and identification are forceful determinants of the
acquisition and development of prosocial behavior. Nurturance is also an important antecedent *if* it is a part of a complex
of parent–child interactions that include modeling. Reasoning with children (induction) is conducive to the development
of prosocial orientations, while parental control by force or
power tends to counteract this development. High maturity
demands on the child and early assignment of responsibility
for others stimulate the acquisition of prosocial tendencies.

Clearly, these child-rearing practices are not independent
of each other, even though, for research purposes, they are

generally examined one at a time. For instance, parents who reason with their child instead of forcing obedience are more apt than others to serve as models of prosocial behavior and to elicit strong identifications from their child. There is an urgent need to explore the interrelationships among these practices and to determine the effects of combinations or patterns of disciplinary techniques on children's prosocial behavior.

Finally, it should be noted that there are many other dimensions of child-rearing whose consequents for prosocial behavior have not yet been adequately researched—permissiveness, democracy in decision-making, imposition of restrictive rules, family cohesiveness, preaching and lectures by parents, and many others. Which of these techniques or family patterns are effective in promoting altruism and consideration among children, and which inhibit the development of prosocial orientations? To date, there are no systematic data and, consequently, no adequate answers to these questions.

The Mass Media
as Socializers

Because parents are the primary and most significant agents of socialization, their relationships with their children have been the subject of considerable research. The last chapter summarized compelling evidence that parental modeling and the use of certain kinds of child-rearing techniques have clear and substantial impacts on the development of prosocial behavior.

But parents are not the only agents of socialization. Peers, teachers, priests, ministers, and neighbors also serve in this capacity, and they undoubtedly help mold the child's behavior, motives, attitudes, and orientations. Yet, there has been surprisingly little systematic investigation of their actual influence on children's prosocial tendencies.

As might be anticipated, peers often model actions—approved as well as disapproved—that children copy. There is abundant evidence on copying peers' aggressive behaviors, and there are clear and definite data on the effects of peer models on prosocial behavior.[1] Children, particularly boys, are likely to emulate what they observe peers doing, including donating to charity, expressing sympathy, or helping someone in distress.[2] Clearly, peers can be powerful models in the acquisition and modification of prosocial responses of children. Repeated exposure to prosocial peer models might be expected to induce strong, generalized, and enduring prosocial dispositions in the same way that repeated exposure to adult prosocial models does (see p. 79). Unfortunately, this plausible inference has not been tested empirically, but, on the basis of the accumulated evidence, we would guess that it is valid.

Similarly, teachers' rewards, punishments, and modeling must influence their pupils' behavior. The adult models in one study who acted as the children's caretakers in nursery school (and were probably perceived as teachers) were highly effective in eliciting imitation of their altruistic behavior (see p. 82). However, to the best of our knowledge, there are no systematic investigations of teachers' modeling of prosocial conduct in naturalistic, classroom settings—another problem for future research.

Characters in the mass media, particularly television, also serve as models to be identified with and imitated. This hardly seems surprising in view of the fact that children and adolescents spend more time watching television than in any other single activity but sleep. It is therefore quite possible that television viewing may have greater impact on children's lives than school does. Children cannot avoid learning from television. As Nicholas Johnson, formerly commissioner of the Federal Communications Commission, put it: "All television is educational television. The only question is, what is it teaching?"[3]

After an excellent review of the effects of television viewing, three experts on children's television noted:

> The medium ... is a powerful force which operates through observational learning, itself a natural process which is continually at work in the lives of our children. Thus, technology has given us a uniquely potent teacher—and in a complex society like our own, effective teachers are much needed. At the same time, though, the greater the power of the teacher, the greater is its capacity to work for either good or harm.[4]

Concern with the welfare of children and television's potentially harmful effects has stimulated a tremendous amount of controversy, protest, and, fortunately, research about the influence of television. The principal focus of the research has been on the effects of the pervasive violence and aggression of television programs. Numerous studies of the topic clearly and uniformly confirm that the effects of television are extremely forceful and that television characters are taken as models; children imitate the aggressive behavior they witness on the television screen.[5] There is indisputable evidence that aggressive behaviors are directly acquired from television programs, and retained. Children become more aggressive in behavior and attitudes following exposure to television violence, and these effects are both immediate and long-term.[6] Violence on television, even cartoon violence, may also have negative effects on children's prosocial responses, reducing cooperation and sharing with peers.[7]

Since television has such striking general effects on aggression, it must also have great potential for stimulating the development of prosocial behavior. Some behavioral scientists have turned their attention to this issue, and, although research in this area is in its incipient phases, there are already some encouraging findings.

Prosocial Television
and Children's Behavior

Television characters who perform (model) prosocial actions
(helping others, offering nurturance and sympathy, sharing)
are emulated by children-viewers.[8] Some of the most extensive
and salient research on this subject was conducted by Friedrich and Stein.[9] They examined the effects of various types of
prosocial television programs on preschool pupils between the
ages of three and five. Children were shown one of three types
of television programs each day for four weeks: aggressive
cartoons (Batman and Superman); prosocial shows (Mister
Rogers' Neighborhood, a program in which there are many
displays of cooperation, sympathy, sharing, understanding
the feelings of others); or films with neutral content. Naturalistic observations were made in the classroom before, during,
and after the period during which the programs were shown.
Aggressive children (those initially above the median in aggression) became less able to tolerate delays and more dis-
obedient to rules after exposure to the aggressive programs,
but those who were initially nonaggressive (below the median)
did not become more aggressive.

Exposure to prosocial television programs resulted in positive changes in behavior, such as greater persistence at tasks,
more obedience to school rules, and greater ability to tolerate
delays. Most important from our point of view were the gains
in levels of cooperation, nurturance, and sympathy, as well as
in verbalization of their own and others' feelings, among
children of lower socioeconomic status. These effects were still
discernible two weeks later. Unexpectedly, some children
from higher socioeconomic levels showed *increased* prosocial
behavior after exposure to the aggressive and neutral pro-

grams. Further investigation revealed that these children habitually watched fewer aggressive programs than their peers, and the investigators argue that the fast-moving, noisy, aggressive programs stimulated their social activity, which was reflected in increased prosocial behavior.[10]

The positive effects of viewing prosocial behavior can be enlarged by training following the television viewing. This was demonstrated in a study in which kindergarten children were assigned to one of five treatments for four sessions: (1) prosocial television programs and verbal-labeling training; (2) prosocial television programs and training in role-playing; (3) prosocial television programs plus verbal labeling *and* training in role-playing; (4) prosocial television programs plus irrelevant training; (5) neutral television programs and irrelevant training. Verbal labeling consisted of group discussion of the events similar to those portrayed in the program and of the feelings and actions of the participants. In role-play training, the children manipulated puppets enacting events and dialogue similar to those in the program. The irrelevant activity assigned to the controls groups was playing with commercial games.

To evaluate the effects of the various training experiences, the investigators tested the children's learning of the content of the programs, generalization of the learning to other situations resembling those portrayed in the program, and actual helping behavior (assisting in repairing another child's collage that had been damaged).

As predicted, exposure to prosocial programs has positive effects. Furthermore, both kinds of additional training, verbal labeling and role-playing, enhanced learning and had broad generalization effects, resulting in increased helping in a situation that was far different from that modeled on television.

The labeling training in itself was not effective in raising boys' helping behavior, but when added to role-playing, it further augmented the girls' tendencies to assist another.

The results are notable and have wide social implications, for they indicate that several forms of prosocial interactions can be stimulated by prosocial television programs, even with relatively short exposures. The investigators drew their conclusions carefully and were willing to extrapolate from the laboratory findings to naturalistic settings.

> The clear effects of television and training in this relatively small-scale study suggest that this type of prosocial television can have a strong impact on children who watch it in naturalistic contexts where viewing can occur over a much longer period of time than 1 week. These results appear to be readily applicable to naturalistic settings because the children generalized both learning and behavior to situations quite different from those to which they were exposed in the television and training, and because this generalization occurred in measures administered 2 or 3 days after the television viewing.[11]

Additional extensive effects of exposure to prosocial television have been noted in other recent studies. In one, nursery school children were observed during and after four days of exposure to either Sesame Street, a program in which the characters reinforce others positively and negatively, or Mister Rogers' Neighborhood in which there is a great deal of prosocial behavior and very few punishments. Viewing Mister Rogers' Neighborhood proved to be very effective in augmenting children's prosocial behavior; after viewing this program children initiated more social contacts and reinforced their peers more frequently, that is, they offered more praise and approval, sympathy, affectionate physical contact, and emotional support.

Watching Sesame Street produced more complicated results but, in general, led to intensification of behaviors that
were initially of low frequency. Thus, children who originally
gave little positive reinforcement to peers were likely to give
more reinforcement after exposure to Sesame Street; those
who were originally low in punitiveness became more
punitive.[12]

These impacts are not restricted to children of nursery
school age. Some of the first graders in one study were shown
an episode from the Lassie series in which a boy risked his life
to save a dog, and others were shown either a Lassie episode
without such altruism or a family situation comedy. Subsequently, each child had an opportunity to come to the aid of
some distressed puppies, but only at some cost—helping the
puppies meant giving up a game in which the child could win
a valuable prize. The children who had seen the altruistic
Lassie episode gave substantially more help to the puppies in
distress than did the children exposed to either of the other
programs.[13]

The overwhelming weight of the evidence supports the
hypothesis that exposure to television programs that model
prosocial behavior enhances children's prosocial tendencies.
These findings come from studies that made use of actual
television programs and involved heroes that were generally
known to the children, and further confirmation is found in
studies using films especially created for research. Children
who were exposed to generous models in these specially designed films donated more of the prizes they had won to needy
children than did those who witnessed stingy models.[14]

The uniformity in the findings from diverse studies leave no
doubt that the impacts of television viewing are profound and
pervasive. The effects can be positive, enhancing prosocial

behavior, or negative, reducing prosocial behavior and increasing antisocial responses, depending on the people and events portrayed and the behavior modeled. It is inevitable that we draw a moral from these frequently replicated research findings, and we cannot ignore that moral. Given television's potential for promoting prosocial behavior, we must ask what keeps it from doing so. After an extensive review of virtually all the relevant literature on the topic, Liebert, Neale, and Davidson argue that the answer to that question lies, to a considerable degree, in "the commercial structure of television and its influence on program content."[15] They point out that as consumers, concerned citizens are in an excellent position to pressure advertisers to alter their programs by refusing to purchase the products of advertisers whose programs promote violence and by patronizing those who sponsor prosocial performances.

The reader may not agree with their analyses of why the positive, prosocial potential of television is unrealized, or with their recommendations for remedying the situation. But it is difficult to disagree with their final conclusion and advice:

> It behooves us, in a world on the brink of disaster, to harness television's potential to contribute to our society in ways which we deem more desirable. All of us must bear the responsibility for what is being taught on television. Accepting it squarely can lead to programming which serves the highest values of society—a medium which is truly in the public interest. In the past, children have seen and learned violence on TV's window and today they continue to do so. In the future they might, instead, learn constructive solutions to the problems they will face. Which will it be? The choice is ours.[16]

Cognition,
Moral Judgment,
Role-Taking, and Empathy

Introspections about our own prosocial activities convince us of the significance of their cognitive components. Before we help others, express sympathy or consideration, or donate to charity, we have to perceive and interpret a situation accurately and understand others' feelings and emotions. We must also evaluate their needs and desires and decide which actions will be most effective and beneficial to them. Finally, we must formulate and execute our plans for prosocial action. In short, mature prosocial action involves several fundamental cognitive processes: perception, thinking, reasoning, problem-solving, and decision-making.

The role of cognitive processes in the genesis and development of prosocial behavior is not fully understood. At the earliest stages of cognitive development, children are probably not able to perceive and interpret another individual's needs or distress accurately, nor do they know what to do to help relieve someone else's distress; hence, they cannot act prosocially. What are the cognitive prerequisites of showing consideration or kindness, of sharing or helping? At what stage of cognitive development does the child become capable of accurate perceptions of someone else's feelings? Can special training accelerate the growth of children's understanding of others' needs and emotions? Are intelligent children more likely than unintelligent ones to sympathize with victims of oppression? Does greater maturity of reasoning ability or greater sophistication about moral problems imply stronger tendencies toward prosocial responses? These are the kinds of questions that will be examined in this chapter. As we shall see, there are not many definitive answers. Most pertinent research is concentrated on three broad interrelated cognitive variables: general intelligence, moral reasoning or moral judgment, role-taking, and empathy. It is relatively simple to summarize the research on intelligence and prosocial behavior; the other two variables present much more complicated issues and inevitably require some examination of theoretical issues.

Intelligence and Prosocial Behavior

There appears to be little, if any, direct relationship between performance on intelligence tests, the most widely used measures of general cognitive ability, and predispositions to prosocial behavior. Many different criteria of prosocial behavior and a wide variety of intelligence tests have been used in pertinent studies, and it is usual to find either no association, or only a low positive correlation, between the two sets of variables. Substantial correlations (about .40) between intelligence test scores and prosocial behavior were reported in two studies, one involving naturalistic observations of altruism,[1] the other using sociometric criteria (peer nominations for "most considerate" and "most likely to help").[2] The latter correlation is probably inflated because of a "halo effect," specifically, children's tendency to think of their intelligent peers as possessing many desirable qualities, and therefore to list names of these classmates when they are asked to nominate the ones who are most considerate of others. The positive correlations found in most other studies are so low as to be worthless for prediction. It thus seems reasonable to conclude that level of general intelligence or general cognitive ability has little bearing on children's predispositions toward prosocial behavior.[3]

Moral Reasoning

Although the individual's general intelligence level has very little to do with his or her prosocial behavior, we might expect that his judgments and reasoning about moral issues would affect his tendencies toward prosocial action. It might be argued that, by definition, prosocial conduct must involve altruistic motives and judgments based on consideration for others; "accidental" or unintentional acts that benefit others are not truly altruistic. According to Kohlberg, a leading theorist and researcher in the field of moral judgment, "no observation or categorization of behavior 'from the outside' or 'behavioristically' can define its moral status in any psychologically valid sense."[4]

Common experience and casual observation suggest that moral judgments and moral behavior are not closely connected. People do not always behave in accordance with their moral judgments; almost all of us have encountered individuals who articulate the most noble moral principles but act in self-serving ways.

> The gap between moral reasoning and behavior may yawn wide even in history's moral heroes. Gore Vidal's *Burr* levels this charge against Thomas Jefferson: "Proclaiming the unalienable rights of man for everyone (except slaves, Indians, women and those entirely without property), Jefferson tried to seize the Floridas by force, dreamed of a conquest of Cuba, and after his illegal purchase of Louisiana sent a military governor to rule New Orleans against the will of its inhabitants. . . . It was of course Jefferson's gift at one time or another to put with eloquence the "right" answer to every moral question. In practice, however, he seldom deviated from an opportunistic course, calculated to bring him power.[5]

Unfortunately, investigators of prosocial *behavior*—even those concerned with the forces that shape such behavior—seldom attend directly to the actors' cognitions and motivations. On the other hand, theorists and researchers in the field of moral *judgment* have focused almost exclusively on developmental (age) changes in the form and structure of moral concepts, that is, on the stages in the maturation of moral reasoning and judgment. Consequently, there is a paucity of empirical data relating these cognitive variables to prosocial behavior.

Before examining the few accumulated findings, however, we will make a brief but necessary digression to sketch out the most influential theories of moral reasoning, Piaget's and Kohlberg's. Both of these theorists postulate that moral judgment develops through an invariant sequence of age-related stages. The individual's stage or level of moral judgment is assessed by means of interviews or questionnaires about moral dilemmas and decisions.

Piaget's Theory of Moral Development

No one has had a greater impact on research and theory in the field of cognitive development than Jean Piaget. Although his principal interests are in age changes in logic and thinking, some of his work is devoted to children's concepts of justice and morality. In one of his earliest books, *The Moral Judgment of the Child*[6] Piaget described interviews in which children of different ages were told short stories and questioned about rules, punishment, authority, transgressions, wrongdoing, equality, and reciprocity among people. Children were asked, for example, who was more naughty, a boy who unintentionally gave wrong directions to a man so that he got lost, or a boy who mischievously gave wrong directions to a man who found his way despite the misinformation the boy gave him. Analyses of the responses led Piaget to conclude that there are three successive stages in the development of the understanding of rules, moral judgment, and the sense of justice—the heteronomous, the intermediate, and the autonomous.

The first, labeled either the stage of *heteronomous morality, moral realism,* or *morality of constraint,* is characteristic of children who have not yet achieved the stage of concrete operations, that is, children below the ages of seven or eight. During this stage, the child is *morally realistic;* regarding duty as "self subsistent and independent of the mind, as imposing itself regardless of the circumstances in which the individual may find himself."[7] Rules, obligations, and commands are regarded as "givens," external to the mind, inflexible, and unchangeable. Justice is whatever authority (adults) or the law commands; whatever rewards or punishment authorities give. The good is obedience, and wrongdoing is judged according to the letter, not the spirit, of the law.

The thinking of children at this stage is also characterized by beliefs in *immanent justice* (that Nature will punish trans-gressions) and in the *absoluteness* of the values held—everything is totally right or totally wrong. Furthermore, acts are eval-uated on the basis of their *consequences* rather than of the actor's *intentions* or *motivations.* Severe, arbitrary punishments are favored; the more serious the consequences of an act, the greater the punishment the actor deserves.

According to Piaget, the sources of *moral realism* are the child's cognitive structures and experiences. The principal cognitive factors are general *egocentrism* which is reflected in the child's belief that everyone shares his or her views of events, and *realism of thought,* that is, the tendency to reify psychological phenomena such as thoughts, rules, or dreams, to conceive of them as physical, thing-like entities. The envi-ronmental or experiential factors that foster moral realism are *adult control and constraint,* the inherently unequal relationship between children and parents.

The second stage in the development of moral reasoning begins about the age of seven or eight. At this age the child interacts more extensively with peers and has more egalitar-ian, give-and-take relationships with others. A sense of au-tonomy and egalitarianism becomes prominent, equality begins to take priority over authority in matters of distribu-tion, and beliefs in immanent justice and severe punishments are superseded by ideas of reciprocal punishment (punish-ment fitting the crime).

The third, most mature stage, called *autonomous morality, moral relativism,* or *morality of cooperation,* generally emerges at about eleven or twelve years of age. Equity dominates in the child's thinking about justice; extenuating circumstances, motivations, and intentions weigh heavily in making moral judgments. Egalitarian concepts of justice prevail; arbitrary punishments, immanent justice, moral absolutism, and blind obedience to authority are rejected. Rules are considered to be products of social interaction and therefore changeable.

The achievement of mature, autonomous concepts of justice is, to a large extent, the product of cooperation, reciprocity, and role-taking among peers. In Piaget's view, there are no absolute authority figures in the peer group, and children therefore develop ideas of equality, cooperation, and group solidarity. The child has to assume others' views—to take roles—and, at the same time, discussion and criticism among equals prevails. As a result, the child's egocentrism diminishes, and concern for the welfare and rights of others increases.

According to Piaget, all normal children progress through this hierarchical sequence of stages. Individual differences in rates of progress are due to variations in cognitive maturity, opportunities for peer cooperation and reciprocal role-taking, moral education, home life, and other environmental factors. Piaget's notion of developmental sequence from heteronomous to autonomous conceptions of justice is confirmed by findings from empirical research. Boys and girls representing a variety of nationalities and races, socioeconomic classes, and intelligence levels go through the same series of stages of moral development.[8]

Kohlberg's Theory of Moral Development

Beginning his work about thirty years later than Piaget, but strongly influenced by his ideas, Lawrence Kohlberg of Harvard University has presented another theory of the development of moral judgments which amplifies Piaget's sequence of stages. Kohlberg's schema was based on analyses

of interviews with boys ranging from ten to sixteen years of
age. In these interviews, he presented a series of moral dilemmas in story form. In each, obedience to laws or to authority
conflicts with the welfare of the actor or other people. The
subject is asked what the hero of the story should do; and this
is followed by a series of questions (probes) about the thinking
underlying the answers.

Here are the best-known story and some of the probes that
go with it:

> In Europe, a woman was near death from a special kind of
> cancer. There was one drug that the doctors thought might save
> her. It was a form of radium that a druggist in the same town
> had recently discovered. The drug was expensive to make, but
> the druggest was charging ten times what the drug cost him to
> make. He paid $200 for the radium and charged $2,000 for a
> small dose of the drug. The sick woman's husband, Heinz, went
> to everyone he knew to borrow the money, but he could only get
> together about $1,000, which is half of what it cost. He told the
> druggist his wife was dying, and asked him to sell it cheaper or
> let him pay later. But the druggist said, "No, I discovered the
> drug and I'm going to make money from it." So Heinz got
> desperate and broke into the man's store to steal the drug for his
> wife.
>
> Should Heinz have done that? Was it actually wrong or right?
> Why? Is it a husband's duty to steal the drug for his wife if he
> can get it no other way? Would a good husband do it? Did the
> druggist have the right to charge that much where there was no
> law actually setting a limit to the price? Why?

Of central importance in assessing moral maturity are the
quality of the judgments, the ways of perceiving the conflict
situation, moral principles and their applications to a number of different kinds of issues (civil liberties, contracts and
promises, punitive justice, personal conscience, issues of
authority, and democracy) rather than the "solutions"
chosen.[9]

According to Kohlberg, children's moral development advances through a sequence of six stages, ordered into three levels of moral orientation. These are summarized and defined in Table 1. The schema is more complex and extensive than Piaget's, and it deals with changes that occur through middle childhood, adolescence, and adulthood. In fact, principled moral reasoning, the highest levels, is characteristic of only a small proportion of mature adults.

The stages are said to be invariant in sequence, hierarchical, universal, and intrinsic to the species, although any particular individual's development may cease at any stage. Each successive stage is seen as qualitatively different from the others, a more advanced "structured whole," embracing a new, more comprehensive, and more coherent cognitive organization of moral thinking.

Like Piaget, Kohlberg asserts that progress from one moral stage to the next is the result of the interaction of the maturation of the organism and experience. The maturation of cognitive capacities is critical because judging right and wrong is primarily an active cognitive process. Social *role-taking* is considered the most influential experiential factor in moral development. Role-taking enhances the individual's ability to empathize with others and to perceive things from others' points of view. By taking roles, the child becomes aware of conflicts or discrepancies between his or her own and others' judgments and actions. The resolution of conflicts between differing points of view brings the individual to higher, more mature moral stages which are more stable than the lower ones.

Some fundamental tenets of Kohlberg's theory have been tested empirically and have been supported. Children from Taiwan, Mexico, Yucatan, and Turkey advance through the same sequence of moral stages as Americans do, thus

TABLE 1 Definition of Kohlberg Moral Stages

I. Preconventional Level

At this level the child is responsive to cultural rules and labels of good and bad, right or wrong, but interprets these labels in terms of either the physical or the hedonistic consequences of action (punishment, reward, exchange of favors), or in terms of the physical power of those who enunciate the rules and labels. The level is divided into the following two stages:

Stage 1: *The punishment and obedience orientation.* The physical consequences of action determine its goodness or badness regardless of the human meaning or value of these consequences. Avoidance of punishment and unquestioning deference to power are valued in their own right, not in terms of respect for an underlying moral order supported by punishment and authority (the latter being stage 4).

Stage 2: *The instrumental relativist orientation.* Right action consists of that which instrumentally satisfies one's needs and occasionally the needs of others. Human relations are viewed in terms like those of the market place. Elements of fairness, of reciprocity, and of equal sharing are present, but they are always interpreted in a physical pragmatic way. Reciprocity is a matter of "you scratch my back and I'll scratch yours," not of loyalty, gratitude, or justice.

II. Conventional Level

At this level, maintaining the expectations of the individual's family, group, or nation is perceived as valuable in its own right regardless of immediate and obvious consequences. The attitude is not only one of *conformity* to personal expectations and social order but of loyalty to it, of actively *maintaining,* supporting, and justifying the order, and of identifying with the persons or group involved in it. At this level, there are the following two stages:

Stage 3: *The interpersonal concordance or "good boy—nice girl" orientation.* Good behavior is that which pleases or helps others and is approved by them. There is much conformity to stereotypical images of what is majority or "natural" behavior. Behavior is frequently

Source: L. Kohlberg, "From Is to Ought: How to Commit the Naturalistic Fallacy and Get Away with It in the Study of Moral Development," in

judged by intention—"he means well" becomes important for the first time. One earns approval by being "nice."

Stage 4: *The "law and order" orientation.*   There is orientation toward authority, fixed rules, and the maintenance of the social order. Right behavior consists of doing one's duty, showing respect for authority, and maintaining the given social order for its own sake.

III.   Postconventional, Autonomous, or Principled Level

At this level, there is a clear effort to define moral values and principles which have validity and application apart from the authority of the groups or persons holding these principles, and apart from the individual's own identification with these groups. This level again has two stages:

Stage 5: *The social-contract legalistic orientation,* generally with utilitarian overtones. Right action tends to be defined in terms of general individual rights, and standards which have been critically examined and agreed upon by the whole society. There is a clear awareness of the relativism of personal values and opinions and a corresponding emphasis upon procedural rules for reaching consensus. Aside from what is constitutionally and democratically agreed upon, the right is a matter of personal "values" and "opinion." The result is an emphasis upon the "legal point of view," but with an emphasis upon the possibility of changing law in terms of rational considerations of social utility (rather than freezing it in terms of stage 4 "law and order"). Outside the legal realm, free agreement and contract is the binding element of obligation. This is the "official" morality of the American government and constitution.

Stage 6: *The universal ethical principle orientation.*   Right is defined by the decision of conscience in accord with self-chosen *ethical principles* appealing to logical comprehensiveness, universality, and consistency. These principles are abstract and ethical (the Golden Rule, the categorical imperative); they are not concrete moral rules like the Ten Commandments. At heart, these are universal principles of *justice,* of the *reciprocity* and *equality* of human *rights,* and of respect for the dignity of human beings as *individual persons.*

Cognitive Development and Epistemology, ed. T. Mischel, New York: Academic Press, 1971.

confirming Kohlberg's hypothesis that the sequence is universal. Subjects in other cultures, particularly in British Honduras and in isolated villages of Yucatan and Turkey, move through the sequence more slowly, however, and very few of them gave evidence of principled reasoning.[10]

The idea that maturity of moral judgment depends upon level of cognitive development is central to Kohlberg's theory. The attainment of a particular stage of thinking and reasoning is considered a necessary, although not sufficient, precondition for the achievement of a parallel stage of moral judgment. The empirical support for this idea is impressive.[11] In addition Kohlberg's hypothesis that role-taking opportunities contribute to the development of moral maturity has been confirmed in a number of experimental and correlational studies.[12]

The theories of Piaget and of Kohlberg have had enormous impact on the field of moral reasoning. Yet, in a sense, both deal with a circumscribed domain of moral reasoning because their data base consists primarily of children's verbalizations about laws, rules, authority, responsibility, equality, and justice. The prosocial domain (the thoughts, concepts, and judgments about issues such as personal sacrifice and conflicts between one's own needs and those of others) is not tapped in Piaget's or Kohlberg's procedures. Consider the moral dilemma of a girl who has to decide between protecting herself and risking her own safety to help someone in distress. There is no a priori reason to believe that the same conceptions, judgments, and principles are applied in resolving this dilemma as in dealing with the dilemmas presented by Piaget and Kohlberg.

Eisenberg presented elementary and high school children with four moral judgment dilemmas concerning prosocial actions and conflicts between one's own and another's desires.[13] One of the dilemmas follows:

> Bob, a young man who was very good at swimming, was asked to help young crippled children who could not walk to learn to swim so that they could strengthen their legs for walking. Bob was the only one in his town who could do this job well because only he had had both life-saving and teaching experiences. But helping the crippled children would take much of Bob's free time left after work and school, and Bob had wanted to practice very hard as often as possible for a series of very important swimming contests coming up. If Bob did not practice swimming in all his free time, his chances of winning the contests, and also for receiving a paid college education or a sum of money, would be greatly lessened.
>
> Should Bob agree to teach the crippled children? Why? [More probes follow.]

Careful analyses of the children's and adolescents' responses to these stories revealed four major age-related states in the development of thinking about prosocial moral issues. These are summarized in Table 2.

Stage 1 reasoning, reflecting hedonistic and pragmatic orientations, was predominant only in the responses of elementary school children. They frequently referred to social approval or stereotyped notions of good and bad behavior in explaining the reasons underlying their solutions to the dilemmas. *Empathic* (Stage 3) reasoning was used most often by high school students, although it appeared in some of the judgments of fourth- and sixth-grade pupils. References to internalized values and norms (including duty, responsibility, and the need to protect the rights of others) governed the reasoning of some high school students, particularly those in the eleventh and the twelfth grade.

The reasoning used in resolving prosocial dilemmas is similar in some respects to that underlying the proposed solutions to dilemmas involving constraints (laws, rules, and obligations). But there are also some major differences in children's thinking about these two domains. Young chil-

TABLE 2   Stages of Prosocial Moral Reasoning

Stage 1: Two uncorrelated types of reasoning are grouped together because both are frequently verbalized by the youngest subjects:

Hedonistic, pragmatic orientation: The individual is concerned with selfish or pragmatic consequences rather than moral considerations. "Right" behavior is that which is instrumental in satisfying the actor's own needs or wants. Reasons for assisting or not assisting another include consideration of direct gain to the self, future reciprocity, and concern for others whom the individual needs and/or likes.

"Needs of others" orientation: The individual expresses concern for the physical, material, and psychological needs of others even though the others' needs conflict with one's own needs. This concern is expressed in the simplest terms, without clear evidence of role taking, verbal expressions of sympathy, or reference to internalized affect such as guilt ("He's hungry" or "She needs it").

Stage 2: *Approval and interpersonal orientation and/or stereotyped orientation:* Stereotyped images of good and bad persons and behaviors and/or consideration of others' approval and acceptance are used in justifying prosocial or non-helping behaviors. For example, one helps another because "it's nice to help" or because "he'd like me more if I helped."

dren's judgments about prosocial moral dilemmas were more advanced than their reasoning about laws, rules, and formal obligations. Thus, in dealing with Kohlberg dilemmas, children of ten or younger resorted principally to Stage 1 reasoning, oriented toward authority and punishment,[14] but this kind of explanation was scarcely apparent among even the youngest subjects (seven years old) solving prosocial dilemmas. Stereotypes of good and bad behavior were invoked at an earlier age in solving prosocial dilemmas than

Stage 3a: *Empathic orientation:* The individual's judgments include evidence of sympathetic responding, role taking, concern with the other's humaness, and/or guilt or positive affect related to the consequences of one's actions. Examples include "I know how he feels," "I care about people," and "I'd feel bad if I didn't help because he'd be in pain."

Stage 3b: *Transitional stage:* Justifications for helping or not helping involve internalized values, norms, duties, or responsibilities, or refer to the necessity of protecting the rights and dignity of other persons; these ideas, however, are not clearly and strongly stated. References to internalized affect self-respect and living up to one's own values are considered indicative of this stage if they are weakly stated. Examples include "It's just something I've learned and feel."

Stage 4: *Strongly internalized stage:* Justifications for helping or not helping are based on internalized values, norms, or responsibilities, the desire to maintain individual and societal contractual obligations, the belief in the dignity, rights, and equality of all individuals. Positive or negative affects related to the maintenance of self respect and living up to one's own values and accepted norms also characterize this stage. Examples of stage 4 reasoning include "I feel I have a responsibility to help other people in need" or "I would feel bad if I didn't help because I'd know that I didn't live up to my values."

in responses to the Kohlberg stories, and empathy played a more significant role in making judgments about prosocial issues. These findings led Eisenberg to conclude that, in general, young children's conceptions and moral judgments regarding prosocial issues are more advanced than their judgments about moral constraints.[15]

Kohlberg's, Piaget's, and Eisenberg's data demonstrate clearly that modes of thinking about moral issues, and conceptualizations of the motives underlying moral decisions,

vary with age and cognitive maturity. Are there corresponding changes with age and cognitive maturity in the motivations and cognitions underlying prosocial conduct? Although
there is a scarcity of information that is directly relevant, some
tenable hypotheses can be formulated and tested. For example, given the data on age changes in moral reasoning, we
might predict that altruism and sharing among nursery
school children are likely to be motivated by expectations of
reward or social approval or adherence to stereotypical notions of "good" and "bad." On the other hand, adolescents'
consideration and kindness are more likely to be based on
empathy and internalized moral principles. These are simply
hypotheses, not facts, and their validity can be assessed only
through systematic research centered on the thought processes
and motivations regulating prosocial behavior. This is an issue
for future research.

Moral Reasoning and Prosocial Behavior

As we noted earlier, we might reasonably hypothesize a
positive, but not strong or direct, relationship between stage
of moral judgment and predispositions to prosocial behavior,
and a number of studies support this hypothesis. Low levels of
moral judgment, assessed by means of the Kohlberg test, have
been found to predict delinquency and cheating in experimental situations;[16] children and adolescents with relatively
mature moral judgment are more likely to manifest more
helping and generosity than peers at lower levels of moral
reasoning.[17] Significant and positive, though moderate, correlations are typical.

Some of the corroborative evidence comes from studies
using techniques like Piaget's; other investigators adapted

Kohlberg procedures. In one, "scores" (level) of boys and girls between the ages of seven and thirteen on a test based on Piaget's stages of moral judgment were found to be significantly related to their generosity (amount of charitability, giving donations). In this group, generosity generally increased with age, just as the level of moral reasoning did, but analysis of the data suggests that age alone did not account for the variability in generosity, ". . . rather the findings may be interpreted as showing that age-related changes in generosity are attributable to developmental transformations in moral judgment."[18] Other data show that the level of moral judgment among five- to eight-year-olds, tested by stories adapted from Piaget's, is positively related to sharing candy with a friend or with strangers.[19]

Adults at higher moral stages (Kohlberg test) were more likely than others to aid someone in distress, even if offering help meant defying an authority's instructions.[20] In another study, seven-year-olds were given an adaptation of the Kohlberg test and had two opportunities to behave altruistically—to donate candy to poor children and to help a younger child complete a task. As predicted, scores on the moral judgment test were positively correlated with both indices of altruism. Since the correlation was significant even after mental age (a measure of general cognitive level) was partialled out, it may be inferred that manifestations of altruism are a function of maturity of moral judgment itself, rather than of general cognitive level.[21]

Finally, the Kohlberg moral maturity measures of boys in the fifth grade (about ten and one-half years of age) were significantly positively correlated with sociometric assessments (peer nominations) of altruism, cooperation, helping, consideration of others, sharing, and defending victims of injustice. The moral maturity measure was most highly correlated with a reputation for being dependable in offering help to others.[22]

We conclude that stage or level of moral judgment is a significant, although not very powerful, regulator of the individual's propensity to behave prosocially. The correlations discovered are not strong enough to permit accurate predictions of any particular individual's behavior, however.

Role-Taking and Empathy

Many theorists maintain that empathy, sharing another's emotional responses, is a prerequisite of prosocial behavior, a motivational process that mediates between perception of others' needs or distress and prosocial acts. In defining empathy, some stress only cognitive components (comprehension of social situations or role-taking ability) while others underscore affective arousal, the matching of one's own feelings and emotions with someone else's. We find Feshbach's comprehensive definition—"shared emotional responses which the child experiences on perceiving another's emotional reaction"[23]—the most satisfactory for it explicitly encompasses both cognitive and affective facets. Specifically, Feshbach's model of empathy contains three components, two cognitive and one affective. The first component, at the most primitive cognitive level, is the *ability to discriminate and label affective states of others.* A second cognitive component, "reflecting a more advanced level of cognitive competence, or social comprehension, is the *ability to assume the perspective and role of another person.* It is as though the observing child is viewing the situation in the same way as the child who is actually experiencing the situation." The third component is *emotional responsiveness:* "The observing child must be able to experience the negative or positive emotion that is being witnessed in order to be able to share that emotion."[24]

Piaget maintains that young children do not have sufficient cognitive maturity to take another's point of view. Until the period of concrete operations (before the age of seven, approximately) children cannot readily "decenter"; they attend to only one dimension of a situation at a time and cannot consider several aspects of a problem or multiple perspectives simultaneously. At this stage, the children are egocentric and capable of considering only their own points of view. In later childhood, during the stage of concrete operations (about seven to twelve years of age), the child can attend to several aspects of a problem at a time and, in addition, considers reciprocal relationships and the viewpoints of others.

Research findings generally support Piaget's postulates. With increasing age, children become less egocentric and more able to adopt another's perspective.[25] Empathy, measured by tests of tendencies to share the feelings and emotions of characters in stories, ordinarily increases between the ages of five and eight.[26]

Theories of Empathy

Many writers consider empathy to be the chief motive for altruism.[27] Aronfreed has offered a detailed learning-theory explanation of the development of empathy which was described earlier. In this view, empathy is acquired early by conditioning or association, that is, by repeated pairing of the child's feelings of pleasure with someone else's expression of the corresponding feelings[28] (see p. 29).

Psychoanalytic theorists hold that empathy develops from the earliest infant–caretaker interactions because the caretaker's moods are communicated to the infant by touch, tone of voice, and facial expressions.[29] Others use the principles of conditioning to explain the significance of the infant–caretaker relationship in the genesis of empathy—especially if the infant is closely attached to the caretaker.

> When baby and mother face a common cause of distress, or when emotional upset in the baby calls forth an empathic response in the mother, then from the baby's point of view, perception of the mother's distress will become conditioned to his own feelings of distress. As a consequence, the later perception of her distress will evoke a similar response in him. We may presume that a good deal of such conditioning goes on in the earlier years (and indeed throughout life). But it is also most likely to occur within a close mother–child attachment, since the devoted mother is constantly mirroring back to her child his own emotional states in an amplified and enriched form. In her efforts to get into tune with him she may well exaggerate her expressions of pleasure or distress in response to his . . . . It is difficult to overestimate the importance of this continual and intimate interaction of mother and child for the development of sensitive empathic responsiveness to others.[30]

In a recent series of papers, Martin Hoffman[31] proposed an intriguing theory of growth and change in altruistic motivation in the early years that emphasizes both the cognitive and affective aspects of empathy.

> The central idea of the theory . . . is that since a fully developed empathic reaction is an internal response to cues about the affective states of someone else, the empathic reaction must depend heavily on the actor's cognitive sense of the other as distinct from himself which undergoes dramatic changes developmentally. The development of a sense of the other . . . interacts with the individual's early empathic responses to lay the basis for altruistic motivation.[32]

Empathic responses—particularly empathic distress, defined as "experiencing another's painful emotional state"— develop early in infancy as a consequence of either built-in

human tendencies toward empathy or early classical conditioning. As a consequence,

> cues of pain or displeasure from another or from his situation
> evoke associations with the observer's own past pain, resulting in
> an empathic affective reaction. A simple example is the child
> who cuts himself, feels the pain, and cries. Later, on seeing
> another child cut himself and cry, the sight of the blood, the
> sound of the cry, or any other distress cue or aspect of the
> situation having elements in common with his own prior pain
> experience can now elicit the unpleasant affect initially asso-
> ciated with that experience.[33]

Hoffman believes that infants are capable of experiencing
empathic distress before they can differentiate themselves
from others. Consequently, they are often unclear about who
is feeling the distress they witness and may, at times, behave as
though what happens to others is happening to them. Psychoanalytic writers also subscribe to this notion.

When the baby acquires a cognitive sense of the other as
distinct from himself, at about one year of age or a little later,
early empathic distress is "gradually transformed into a more
reciprocal, sympathetic concern for the victim" (sympathetic
distress).[34] However, for some time, although aware of others
as separate individuals, the toddler sees the world only from
his or her own perspective and does not realize that others
have their own traits and feelings. Instead, babies attribute
their own feelings to others, and may therefore use inappropriate means in attempting to relieve another's distress. For
example, a thirteen-month-old brought his own mother to
comfort a crying friend, even though the friend's mother was
equally available, and another toddler offered his own favor-
ite doll to cheer up an adult who looked sad.

At about the age of two, the children begin to consider
others as distinct physical entities with their own feelings,
thoughts, and emotions. Some children this age are capable of

rudimentary role-taking and are more highly motivated to "put [themselves] in the other's place and find the true source of his distress."[35] Then they can respond in ways that may relieve the other's distress rather than their own.

Until they are between six and nine years of age, children's empathic responses are restricted to another's immediate, transitory and situation-specific distress. With greater cognitive maturity and awareness of their own and others' continuing existence, children begin reacting to general conditions (including deprivation, oppression, illness, and incompetence) as well as to immediate distress. "With further cognitive development the person may also be able to comprehend the plight not only of an individual but also of an entire group or class of people—such as the economically impoverished, politically oppressed, socially outcaste, victims of war, or mentally retarded."[36]

Hoffman's theory is appealing because it views empathy in a broad developmental perspective, changing with increasing age, advancing cognitive capacities, and the maturation of affective processes. Some aspects of the theory are supported by research, but much of it is speculative, and many postulates are extremely difficult to test empirically. For example, there are no adequate methods of measuring empathy in very young children, an important aspect of the theory.

Research Findings

A major tenet of a number of theories is that empathy and role-playing are critical factors mediating prosocial actions. This idea has been tested systematically and, in our opinion, amply supported.

Tests have been devised to measure affective as well as cognitive aspects of empathy. The simplest cognitive tests are concerned with the ability to discriminate and label others' emotions. A child is told a brief story (for example, a happy child at a birthday party) and then asked to identify the emotions of a story character by selecting from several pictures of faces expressing happiness, anger, or fear. Such tests tap only rudimentary cognitive aspects of empathy—essentially social comprehension—and even very young children perform well. By the age of three, most children differentiate between happy and unhappy expressions, while fear and anger are accurately identified a little later.[37] Not surprisingly, performance on these tests is not related to primary school children's tendencies to share candy and possessions.[38]

Cognitive Role-Taking

Performance on tests of role-taking, a more complex cognitive facet of empathy, is positively associated with prosocial behavior, however. In one relevant investigation, six- and nine-year-old boys were given two role-taking tests. In the first, constructed by Flavell,[39] the child is presented with two boxes; 5 cents is printed on a box containing a nickel and 10 cents is printed on the other which holds a dime. The participant is told that in a few minutes he will be asked to outwit another child in a simple game in which the opponent will be permitted to choose one of the boxes for himself. The object of the game is to prevent the opponent from winning either of the two coins by guessing which of the two boxes will be chosen and removing the money from it. (The children were told that the opponent knew that an attempt would be made to trick him or her.) The participant was questioned about how to go about tricking the opponent. The score for role-taking ability was based on the child's skill in taking the perspective of the opponent.

In the second role-taking procedure, created by Selman, social and moral dilemmas were presented in story form. The following is a revised form of a story involving eight-year-olds.

> Shawn is the best tree climber in the neighborhood. One day while climbing down from a tall tree, he falls off the bottom branch but does not hurt himself. His father sees him fall. He is upset and asks him to promise not to climb trees any more.
>
> Later that day, Shawn and his friends meet Holly. Holly's kitten is caught up in a tree and can't get down. Something has to be done right away, or the kitten may fall. Shawn is the only one who climbs trees well enough to reach the kitten and get it down, but he remembers his promise to his father.[40]

After the story is read, the participants were asked several questions about solving the dilemma. The stage of role-taking ability was indexed in terms of the child's comprehension of the viewpoints of the characters and by his or her conceptions of others' motives and feelings. Performance on the two tests was highly significantly related to one form of altruistic behavior, a willingness to share (anonymously) candy with a needy child ($r = .68$).[41]

Further confirmation of the hypothesized link between empathic ability and prosocial acts was found in a study of seven-year-olds who worked individually with the experimenter[42] in a social communication task. Each member of the pair had an identical set of cards, each card with a different graphic design that was difficult to describe. Although a screen prevented them from seeing each other's cards, the experimenter explained that the idea of the game was to match as many of the subject's and experimenter's cards as possible. Successful matching depended on the child's role-taking ability, that is, his skill in adopting the experimenter's point of view and describing each design in terms of objective, distinctive features. The inability to do this (a failure to understand what the experimenter needed to know to match the cards accurately) indicated a high degree of egocentricity, or a low degree of role-taking ability.

Role-taking ability in this test was significantly correlated with kindness and helping. Children with a high capability in taking the experimenter's point of view—and, concomitantly, low levels of egocentricity—donated substantial amounts of their candy to poor children and gave a great deal of aid to a younger child who had been assigned a difficult task. Those low in role-taking ability (high in communicative egocentricity) donated relatively little of their candy and gave little assistance to younger children who needed it.

In another highly relevant study of altruism, twelve boys and twelve girls in the second and third grades, were carefully and frequently observed in school and on the playground over a two-month period. Observers recorded the children's interactions according to a preplanned set of categories. Each child's altruism score was the proportion of his or her responses that were in the categories *offers help, offers support,* and *suggests responsibly.*[43]

Two role-taking tasks were used to evaluate each child's role-taking ability. The first was the nickel-and-dime game described above (see p. 131). In the second test, the child was presented with a series of seven pictures and asked to make up a story about them. Then three pictures were removed and the child was asked to make up a story that another child would tell about the remaining four pictures. The child's responses to the questions that followed each task revealed his or her ability to assume the perspective of another child. This was the basis for scoring role-taking ability.

As predicted, the measures of role-taking were significantly correlated with the behavioral indices of altruism ($r = .46$). Corroborative evidence was added by finding the role-taking ability was also related to teachers' independent ratings of prosocial behavior, patience, and cooperativeness. This study is particularly notable because of the major criterion of altruism used. Based on repeated observation of children in their natural settings over an extended period, it undoubtedly reflects each child's characteristic behavior better than an artificial, laboratory encounter does.[44]

All the evidence we have reviewed leads us to conclude that, as hypothesized, role-taking ability is a forceful antecedent of prosocial behavior. On balance, this conclusion seems justified although a few recent studies failed to find evidence consistent with it. Two studies conducted in England found no relationship between generosity and role-taking ability in children between seven and thirteen years of age.[45] Nor were there any significant correlations between performance in a variety of role-taking tasks and observational measures of sharing, helping, and comforting in three- to seven-year-old children in the United States.[46] It is difficult to interpret this evidence that contradicts the bulk of the findings. The differences may be attributable, in part, to methodological factors.

Affective Aspects of Empathy

Empathy has been hypothesized to be the basis or chief mediator of altruistic behavior, and this has been persuasively corroborated by the results of an experimental study. Although the participants were young adults, the findings have clear developmental implications.[47]

Each of the sixty participants (the average age of the participants was twenty) was paired with a performer, actually, a confederate of the experimenter, and watched him play a game of roulette. Physiological responses associated with emotional arousal (changes in galvanic skin response, blood pulse volume, and heart rate) were recorded as the participants observed his fate. Because perception of similarities between oneself and someone else is known to be effective in inducing empathy, half of the subjects were told that the performer had values and interests similar to their own; the other half were informed that they had been paired with the performer because they were different from him. In addition, half of the "similar" group and half of the "different" group were informed that the performer received a reward (money) when the roulette ball landed on an even number and a shock (punishment) whenever it landed on an odd number. The other half of the participants believed that they were observing the performer doing simple cognitive and motor tasks without receiving any rewards or punishments.

Those who believed they were like the performer were clearly empathic with him. Their psychophysiological reactions to the rewards or punishments given the performer were strong and definite.

After the first series of trials was completed, additional trials were announced. In these, the participants were informed that they would regulate both the amount of money the performer won and the amount of shock he received. Furthermore, they themselves would win money or receive shocks on these extra trials, the amounts depending on what the performer received: the more favorable the outcome for the performer, the less favorable the outcome for the participant. If the performer received less money, the participant would receive more, and if the former received less shock, the latter was given more. In short, the participants had to choose between benefiting themselves at a cost to the performer or helping him at a cost to themselves. The results were clear-cut: the subjects who were most empathic with the performer were highly altruistic toward him, most willing to help him even though this entailed self-sacrifice. These results are entirely congruent with the hypothesis that empathic reactions (including their physiological correlates) mediate altruistic acts.

It has been suggested that physiological arousal may be a critical element in instigating helpful activity.[48] The reasoning is as follows: seeing someone else in distress arouses the observer's physiological reactions which have both cognitive and affective consequents, including evoking disgust, empathy, the norm of helping. If there is continued observation of distress, the arousal becomes more intense and more unpleasant, with the result that the observer is motivated to relieve the other's distress so that his own tensions and discomforts will be reduced. The merits of this suggestion must be evaluated by empirical testing. It does not seem likely that *physiological arousal* is a necessary or sufficient precondition for most helping acts.

Among adolescents, as well as adults, the level of empathic ability is related to helping behavior. High school students responded to an empathy questionnaire in which they rated degree of agreement (from "strongly agree" to "disagree") with each of thirty-three items such as "It makes me sad to see a lonely stranger in a group" and "I get very angry when I see someone being ill treated." Those who scored high in empathy were more likely than others to volunteer to help a researcher in a boring task, an altruistic response to the investigator's request.[49] Studies with adults yield comparable results, showing positive relationships between scores in tests of empathy and kindness to others.[50]

Empathy Training and Altruism

The consistency in the outcomes of these studies, based on populations of different ages and using a variety of criteria and assessment techniques, is compelling evidence that there is a direct link between empathy and prosocial actions. If, as we believe, the predisposition to empathic responses is an acquired capacity, it must be trainable, that is, levels of empathy can be raised by special training. And since empathy is a powerful determinant of prosocial behavior, an increase in empathic ability should be reflected in increments in prosocial actions. These results have been achieved in experimental studies through practice in role-taking.

In one study, kindergarten children were instructed to play the roles of both helper and someone in need of help in several situations (for example, a child falling and hurting herself).[51] Thus the children were trained to understand and express the feelings of altruists and of individuals in distress or need.

The day after this training, each child was observed playing alone in a playroom. At some point, cries of distress (actually, a recording) came from an adjoining room; the child's reactions, observed through a one-way mirror, were recorded. Girls who had practiced role-taking responded to these distress signals significantly more frequently than the controls who did not have this training. Role-playing also had some generalized effects: Boys trained in this skill shared more than controls, even though there was no special training in sharing. Furthermore, these effects were enduring, at least over the short interval of one week.[52]

In another training experiment, six- and nine-year-old boys met in groups of five, all the same age, for twenty-five minutes a day for ten days. In one of the role-taking training tasks, each boy enacted a role in a skit involving all five boys. For example, in one of the skits a boy discovered that he did not have enough tickets to invite all his friends to a football game and so had to decide which friend to eliminate. Each child played one of the roles, either that of the boy himself, or of one of the friends. During the training sessions, the experimenter asked questions that directed each boy's attention to the motives, feelings, and thoughts of the character whose role he was assigned ("Why did you do that?" "How do you feel?). In another experimental group, the boys were instructed to switch roles as the story progressed in order to play a variety of roles so that they would gain several perspectives. A control group met with the experimenter for the same length of time and discussed the stories but had no role-taking experiences. The training had significant effects on the altruistic behavior (sharing candy) of the six-year-old participants. Role-switching led to more sharing than training in a single role, but both kinds of experiences produced more sharing than the control condition.[53]

The pattern of results emerging from these studies of empathy and prosocial behavior, both correlational and experimental, leads us to conclude that (1) the individual's level of empathy is a potent factor governing his or her tendencies to behave prosocially and (2) the capacity for empathy can be strengthened substantially by training and experience. In our view, empathic responses are a necessary, although not sufficient, precondition for prosocial behavior. The question of how empathy, once it is aroused, becomes translated into prosocial action has not yet been adequately answered. It poses an important problem for future research.

Situational
Determinants

CHAPTER

9

It is a psychological truism that all behavior is a function of the interaction between the person and the situation he or she encounters. All our actions are regulated jointly by characteristics residing in us—personality traits, motives, needs, and cognitive abilities—and by the specific, immediately present circumstances or social contexts. A major argument of this book is that there are some impressive consistencies, across situations and over time, in individuals' prosocial behavior. These are largely the products of enduring, internalized qualities, predispositions, and orientations that are shaped by socialization experiences, the capacity for empathy, role-taking ability, and the stage of moral development. In our view, individual differences in these personal characteristics account, to a considerable extent, for the differential reactions of children (or adults) to the same stimulus situation (for example, to seeing someone in distress or receiving an appeal for charity).

At the same time, it is obvious that sometimes the immediate situational context (environmental circumstances and
events, including casual, brief encounters and moods) and
things that "just happen" determine our reactions. In the
literature of social psychology and personality, the term *situational determinants* is used to designate two kinds of impacts:
(1) unique events that radically alter an individual's personality pattern, life style, or propensities toward prosocial behavior and (2) temporary external conditions, singular (or
seldom-repeated) experiences, transient feelings, moods, or
affects that ordinarily have immediate but short-lived effects.
(Situational determinants of the second category may also
have lasting or delayed effects, however, as we shall see.)

An excellent example of the first kind of situational determinant is found in Victor Hugo's brilliant psychological novel
Les Miserables.[1] Jean Valjean, the hero of the novel, is a
former convict who is befriended by a bishop from whom he
steals some silver. When Valjean is captured by the police, the
kind bishop declares that he had given him a gift of the silver,
and Valjean is set free. This one unexpected and overwhelming act of kindness changes Valjean's life completely; he
becomes an extraordinarily generous, considerate, and charitable man who devotes his life to aiding the poor and victims
of injustice. Essentially, the hero had gone through a con-
version experience and began to feel that "if he were not
henceforth the best of men, he would be the worst. That he
must now ascend higher than the bishop or sink lower than
the galley slave, that if he wished to be good he must become
an angel and if he wished to remain wicked, he must become
a monster."

This dramatic fictional account of the impact of a singular
event on an individual's life has parallels in the biographies
of some outstanding exemplars of prosocial behavior.
Mahatma Gandhi, internationally renowned for his self-

sacrifice in the cause of human rights, made the decision to devote his life to the betterment of the welfare of India's millions of downtrodden, and unjustly treated "untouchables" after an event in which he was himself the victim of race prejudice. As a young lawyer working in South Africa, Gandhi refused to travel in a section of a train designated for "coolies or coloreds" (as Indians are classified in South Africa) and was put off the train. From that time on, he devoted all his considerable intelligence and energy to the cause of India's millions both in Africa and in India.[2]

Such dramatic conversions are not very common, but many of us have known of cases of individuals who suddenly decide to dedicate themselves to the pursuit of prosocial goals. A high school student uncertain about her future vocation may "just happen" to attend a lecture given by a charismatic civil rights worker who is passionate about her own work, and persuasive about the need for help in this area. Such a unique episode may alter the adolescent's whole scheme of values, directing her toward total involvement in work in behalf of human rights and welfare.

Such radical shifts in goals and behavior are rare and difficult to study; antecedents can be explored only by retrospective accounts. Are such shifts really as sudden and drastic as they seem or are they precipitated by a single event because the individual is somehow "ready" for this change? Do the shifts, when they occur, entail complete restructuring of cognitions and affects, as well as motivations? Perhaps systematic studies of biographies and autobiographies of individuals who have undergone such conversions can throw light on such questions. But at present radical changes in social orientation and prosocial actions are very little understood.

Casual observation attests that situational determinants of the second type (the immediate social context, transitory events, or temporary conditions) often induce or deter the expression of prosocial tendencies. Intrapersonal variability in prosocial behavior, or variations in the individual's reactions from time to time and from situation to situation, can be understood only by examining the immediate situational contexts the actor encounters. Even the most hard-hearted are likely to assist an elderly companion who has tripped and fallen and will go to the aid of a blind woman having difficulty crossing the street. And few would avoid helping a distressed, screaming toddler who had waded into shallow water, was knocked down by a wave, and was in danger of being swept farther into the sea.

Studies of the effects of situational determinants on prosocial behavior center on less dramatic events or circumstances, but they leave no doubt that some stimuli are generally more effective than others in eliciting prosocial responses. For example, as we shall show in greater detail below, good moods are conducive to prosocial conduct, while negative moods tend to mitigate prosocial tendencies (see p. 144).

The situational determinants that have been investigated most thoroughly are moods, reinforcement, and preaching. We shall discuss research on each of these in some detail. Before beginning the discussion, however, we want to make it explicit that we used very conservative criteria in categorizing variables as situational determinants. We considered a variable (reinforcement, preaching) to be in this category if the evidence about its effects came from manipulations by an experimenter in a controlled laboratory situation on only one, or very few, occasion(s). In most cases, the effects of these manipulations were assessed immediately afterward, although in some cases delayed or longer term effects were also assessed. As we shall see, reinforcements for prosocial behavior, and exposures to preaching, sometimes produce increments in children's helping and donating. The safest conclusion to be drawn from these findings is that the experimental manipulations were successful in promoting prosocial behavior.

Of course, many investigators maintain that their manipulations are analogues or parallels of events that occur frequently in everyday natural settings, at home and in school. They therefore believe that the findings from their experiments can be extrapolated or generalized to real life situations, and, if they are correct, the variables they work with might be considered socialization determinants. Recall our earlier discussion of modeling (see p. 79). We opened that discussion with accounts of experiments in which children were exposed to models who were unfamiliar to them and whom they observed performing some act only once or, at most, on a few occasions. Such brief modeling, if effective in inducing alterations in children's behavior, might be classed a situational determinant. However, we chose to put modeling into the category of socialization determinants instead because we judged some of the experiments on modeling to be accurate representations or analogues of what happens in everyday situations in home and in school. Most importantly, studies of modeling and identification in the natural home environment yielded findings congruent with those derived from laboratory studies. In other words, generalizations of the results from the modeling experiments to the home situation seem to be justified; for this reason, we included modeling in the category of socialization determinants.

Analogously, many other findings reviewed in this chapter seem to be applicable to the natural contexts of socialization. Can we make valid generalizations from experimental results—the consequences of one brief exposure to a particular set of circumstances—to home and school situations? If, for example, the experimental induction of good moods advances children's prosocial tendencies, will a parent's or a teacher's efforts to improve the child's moods have comparable, or even more pronounced, positive effects?

It is quite possible that the answer to these questions is affirmative. But we cannot be sure of this until there is more compelling supportive evidence, evidence based on direct tests of the consequences of applications of these techniques in the natural environment. In the absence of this kind of direct and compelling evidence, we take a conservative, cautious stance, categorizing the variables discussed in this chapter as situational determinants rather than as techniques of socialization.

Moods

Transient moods, including feelings of success and failure, may have substantial effects on both children's and adult's prosocial behavior; people more readily assist others and share possessions when they feel happy, pleased, or successful.[3] To illustrate, in one study the moods of three groups of children, seven to eight years of age, were manipulated by giving them different instructions. The children in one group were instructed to reminisce for a few minutes about happy events in their lives, while those in a second group were to think about sad events, and a third (control) group simply counted numbers for the same length of time. All of them then had a chance to share anonymously with other children some of the money they had earned by participating in the study. Those who had thought about happy events and were presumably enjoying positive affect were more generous (shared more of the money) than the controls or the children who had been concentrating on sad events.[4]

In another study, some fourth graders were led to believe that they had done very well in a bowling game, while others were led to believe that they had not succeeded. Soon afterward, a stranger entered the room and asked for donations to a charity. The children who had experienced success and were in a good mood contributed significantly more than those in control or failure conditions.[5]

Generalizations about the effects of positive moods and feelings of success on prosocial behavior must be qualified, however. Experiments show that young children who are convinced that they have earned and deserve their rewards because they performed well in a game or task do not donate as generously from their winnings as children who do not believe that they deserve their rewards.[6] Under competitive conditions, especially those entailing comparisons of performances, the effects of success on sharing are also likely to be attentuated. Children who were successful at competitive games did not donate more generously than nonwinners when the potential beneficiaries of the donation were peers who also played the games but failed to do well.[7]

The effects of transient positive moods on prosocial behavior are apparently ephemeral. The adult participants in one study were given a gift that presumably elicited positive affects and then were asked to help a stranger. Their willingness to help another increased immediately after the gift was received, but this reaction declined with time even within a very short interval and disappeared within twenty minutes; those who were asked to help twenty minutes after receiving the gift were no more helpful than control groups who had not received gifts.[8]

The reasons for the association between positive affects and increased generosity are not clear, but some explanatory hypotheses have been suggested. According to one, the induced positive affects generalize to become positive attitudes toward the self and others, including elevated feelings of one's own competence and, consequently, reduction in the need to retain all resources for oneself.[9] Another hypothesis is that positive affects induced by gifts or earnings may lead the recipient to feel that these are greater than he or she deserves; this may result in attempts to restore equity by donating generously to others.[10] A third hypothesized explanation is based on the assumption that most of us have incorporated the norm of responsibility, and, consequently, feelings of happiness, competence, or advantages over others obligate us to make sacrifices for others.[11] None of these interesting hypotheses have been adequately tested.

Since positive affects often lead to increased generosity, it might be expected that negative affects would diminish the individual's tendencies to share and help. Experimental investigations yield equivocal or inconsistent results, however; apparently this expectation is met only sometimes and under certain conditions. In some studies, children became less helpful and generous after experiencing failure or contemplating sad events, particularly if their actions occurred in an anonymous situation, that is, if the experimenter did not know whether or not they donated or helped others.[12] But in others, children who felt unhappy or unsuccessful, either because they failed in a task or thought about unpleasant events, did not differ from children in a control group in helping or sharing with others.[13] And, under some circumstances, negative affects actually increased children's sharing when the experimenter was present; children who failed at a task were more likely to help others. Presumably, the children believed that the loss of status associated with the failure could be compensated for by prosocial behavior, thus elevating the child's lowered status in the eyes of the experimenter.[14]

The bulk of the evidence suggests that feelings of sadness and failure generally diminish, rather than increase, generosity among children. This contrasts sharply with the finding that, among adults, negative moods or events frequently lead to increments in prosocial behavior.[15] To explain this difference, Cialdini, Darley, and Vincent[16] have proposed a *negative state relief hypothesis* which holds that during the course of socialization we learn that altruistic or charitable acts can relieve negative self-evaluations that stem from guilt, insults, or embarrassment. Altruistic and cooperative actions are frequently associated with approval and other rewards as we are growing up, so that prosocial tendencies are gradually internalized and acquire secondary reinforcement value. Young children have not yet internalized this reward value, and, consequently, they do not ordinarily help or share with others simply to reduce negative affects.

Support for this hypothesis came from a study in which children of three age groups (six to eight, ten to twelve, and fifteen to eighteen years of age) were instructed to think of depressing personal experiences while control groups thought about neutral events.[17] Subsequently the subjects were given an opportunity to donate the coupons they had earned to peers who did not have a chance to win prizes. As predicted from the hypothesis, the youngest subjects donated less when they felt depressed, the ten- to twelve-year-olds who felt sad donated the same amounts as children who did not think about sad events, and the oldest group donated more when they were sad.

Reinforcements

Rewards or reinforcements may function to elicit, sustain, or increase prosocial behavior. Reinforcement comes in several varieties: material reinforcement (candy, trinkets, or other prizes), social reinforcement (praise or approval), vicarious reinforcement (reinforcement to a model who performs some prosocial act) and vicarious internalized, affective reinforcement.

Children's helping and sharing increases when these responses are directly rewarded or reinforced. If preschool children are given material rewards (bubblegum, for instance) after they have donated something (marbles given to them by the experimenter) to a peer, they are likely to make further donations when given another opportunity, if the experimenter is again in the room.[18]

The principles of behavior modification, essentially consisting of rewarding responses in order to increase their strength or frequency, have been applied with striking results in augmenting children's cooperation.[19] In one classic study, pairs of children between seven and twelve years of age were given reinforcements for simultaneously inserting a stylus into one of three holes in an apparatus. Children responded to the reward and cooperated more readily when they were individually rewarded for these synchronous responses; cooperation decreased when these rewards were withdrawn.[20] Learning to cooperate in motor tasks did not generalize to greater cooperation in social situations. However, one investigator found that children between three and six and one-half who learned cooperative responses in motor tasks through reinforcement were subsequently more friendly and less hostile during free play periods, more concerned with common goals and activities, and more interested in social interactions with other children. Controls who did not learn cooperative motor responses displayed significantly less of these outgoing friendly responses.[21]

Another more recent laboratory study demonstrated that helping and donating behavior may be strengthened through aversive conditioning procedures in which an undesirable response is weakened or eliminated (extinquished) by punishment. The participants were children between eight and ten years of age who initially had low rates of donating to a peer. These children played a marble game, earning pennies that could be exchanged for prizes; the more pennies they earned, the better the prize they could obtain. During their play, they were given repeated opportunities to help a peer by donating a penny to him when a yellow "Help" light appeared. During the training, fines were imposed for failure to donate or to help, and the children were informed of the contingency (association) between the fine and the failure to donate. Under these conditions, the children soon learned to donate pennies to help the other child. Moreover, they continued donating even after the fines were no longer imposed, even though the donating was costly to them, that is, entailed further loss of pennies exchangeable for prizes (unless the experimenter explicitly informed them that the fines were eliminated). The authors concluded that "a self-sacrificial response was instated through an avoidance training procedure."[22]

An experimenter's praise of preschool children for sharing can also lead to greater sharing subsequently.[23] Middle-class preschool children appear to respond more strongly to praise than those of the lower class,[24] but the effects may be only temporary and discernible only when the experimenter is present. Thus, preschool children who won pennies in a marble game gave greater donations to other children after they were praised for sharing, but most of them ceased sharing when the praise was discontinued.[25] At present, there is no evidence that these prosocial responses are generalized to situations in which the experimenter is not present or to different settings.

Nevertheless, on balance, the evidence supports the learning theory hypothesis that rewards and punishments are potent factors in raising or lowering the levels of children's helping and donating actions. The results of the experimental studies have some obvious, practical implications. Rewards for prosocial acts in natural settings (in the home and school) probably have consequences comparable to those found in the laboratory. While that seems to be an indisputable conclusion, we know of no studies that examine directly parental (or teacher) practices in rewarding or punishing prosocial responses. Such studies are needed to assess the extent to which we can generalize from the experimental studies. In addition, the studies could provide information about the conditions (for example, the form, frequency, and timing) that amplify or reduce the effectiveness of rewards in naturalistic settings in promoting prosocial behavior.

Vicarious Reinforcement

Bandura, the leading proponent of social learning theory, argues that "There is considerable evidence ... that the behavior of observers can be substantially modified as a function of witnessing other people's behavior and its consequences for them. Observation of rewarding consequences generally enhances similar performances whereas witnessing punishing outcomes has an inhibiting effect on behavior."[26] Presumably, vicarious reinforcement serves to give the observer information about the probable consequences of the behavior being modeled.

Vicarious reinforcement does not always result in the modification of altruism and generosity, however. In fact, at least two studies failed to find the predicted effects of vicarious social reinforcement for generosity.[27] On the other hand, other studies indicate that explicit manifestations of positive affects accompanying prosocial acts (statements like "This is really fun" or "I feel wonderful") induce substantially more imitation of generous (donating) and helping responses.[28] Furthermore, the effects may be lasting ones.[29]

Preaching

In naturalistic settings, at home, in school, and in church, parents and other models frequently preach while they perform prosocial acts. Is preaching effective in augmenting children's prosocial behavior? According to the results of several experiments, it has considerably less effect than a model's action. In one study of generosity, for example, some girls in the second, third, and fourth grades saw videotapes of a model who donated generously to a charity while she preached selfishness, making statements like "I don't think we should give to crippled children. I hope the kids watching don't." Other girls were exposed to stingy models who preached charity, making statements like "I think that we should give to the crippled kids. I hope the kids watching will." Others observed generous or selfish models whose statements were congruent with their actions, giving generously and preaching generosity or behaving selfishly and preaching greed. The model's practice, what she *did,* determined how the children behaved later on in a similar situation; the model's preaching did not affect the children's behavior.[30] From these results, replicated in other studies,[31] it was concluded, "if the model behaves charitably, so will the child—even if the model has preached greed. And conversely, if the model preaches charity, but practices greed, the child will follow the model's behavior and will not contribute to the charity. Behavior in this area is mainly influenced by behavior, not by words."[32]

The ineffective preaching in these studies was mild and innocuous; in some cases, the models were filmed rather than "live." More direct and forceful preaching, however, can have powerful and enduring effects.[33] According to the findings of one study, for example, a live model's preaching that included explicit normative expectations ("We *should* share our tokens

with Bobby.") had no *immediate* effects on the altruism (donation of tokens) of seven- to eleven-year-old children but had
substantial impact on the child's donations *eight weeks later* in a
somewhat different situation.[34] In this study, the effective
preaching was aimed directly at the children, and the
model-preacher was an important and powerful person, in
this case, a potential future teacher in the school.

More direct and intense exhortations with richer content—
long emotional "sermons" emphasizing the beneficial effects
of donating for both giver and recipient—also raised levels of
fifth graders' generosity.[35] This effect was evident immediately
after the preaching, lasted ten days, and was generalized to
increased donations under quite different conditions.

The most persuasive demonstration of the positive effects of
preaching comes from a study designed to test whether
preaching itself is as effective as modeling in fostering charitability. One group of participants, seven- to ten-year-old boys
and girls, observed a model who played a bowling game, won
tokens, and donated half his winnings to charity. Another
model also played the game, won tokens, and announced that
he would donate half his winnings, because "They expect us to
give some to the poor children; that's what one had better do.
One should keep half for himself . . . and [donate] half for the
poor children. . . ." However, although this model preached
charity, he never modeled it because he was called away
immediately after he did his preaching, before he had a
chance to make a donation. Nevertheless, the children who
observed this model donated as much to charity as the children who observed the model who made donations. In other
words, under some conditions, preaching can be as effective as
the modeling.[36]

Our overall conclusion is that mild, low intensity preaching
is not likely to alter children's prosocial behavior, but more

intensive and direct preaching, with strong arguments favoring prosocial action, may be highly effective. Again, it is tempting to generalize from these findings to the effects of preaching in naturalistic settings, drawing conclusions about applications of the research results to child-rearing and educational practice. But, as we have warned on other occasions, the validity of such generalizations or inferences can only be established by direct investigations.

Characteristics
of the Beneficiary

In making decisions about whether or not to help someone or donate to charity, the individual usually considers the characteristics of the potential beneficiary. Most of us will help others we like, friends, and neighbors, and donate to the handicapped, but we are not likely to aid enemies or donate to those we consider unworthy. Adults tend to be altruistic toward those perceived as helpless, dependent, or the victim of circumstances, particularly if the cost of helping is not great.[37] It is assumed that under these circumstances, empathy is evoked and spurs the individual to do something for the other person(s).

Children are also more likely to share with peers who have empathy-inducing characteristics than with others, donating more to a peer who is said to be friendless than to a peer who is not labeled in this way.[38] For adults as well as for children, personalized, individualized potential beneficiaries are more likely to arouse empathy and, consequently, greater sharing and altruism than an abstract beneficiary, such as a "needy child" or "old folks."[39]

How much children will share with, or help, someone else is
at least partially a function of the potential beneficiary's personal characteristics and social relationships. Children more
readily help and share with attractive, well-liked peers than
with those who are not as well liked.[40] Popular children receive
more approval, affection, tokens, and shared toys from peers
than unpopular children do, [41] and nursery school children
who are warm and attentive to peers are also the recipients of
many demonstrations of nurturance from others.[42]

Yet, under some circumstances, the generosity of friends
may not be reciprocated, and non-friends may be treated
better. The nursery school and primary school children in one
study donated *fewer* trinkets to generous friends and gave more
to less generous friends. They reciprocated the actions of
neutral or disliked peers, however, meeting generosity with
generosity, and selfishness with selfishness.[43] These findings
may be interpreted in terms of a gain–loss hypothesis, an
orientation toward increasing interpersonal gains and decreasing losses. It is as though the child reasoned that if a
friend is generous, nothing is gained by giving a great deal in
return; the friendship is secure and therefore reciprocal giving
is not required. But if a friend gave only a few trinkets, the
child gave more in return in order to secure the friendship, to
minimize the probability of losing a friend. A generous gift
from a non-friend may be perceived as an overture to friendship, and giving generously in return may improve the
chances of gaining a friend.[44]

Children's willingness to donate is also influenced by their
conceptions of how deserving the potential beneficiaries are.
The fourth- and fifth-grade boys who participated in one
study won some tokens in a competitive game and could share
their earnings with others. They were less willing to share with
boys who had failed to win tokens and were responsible for
their own failure than with boys who simply had not had an

opportunity to participate.[45] Moreover, children gave more generously to others who claimed they deserved some of the winnings than to those who did not make such statements.[46]

Other Situational Variables

Assignment of Responsibility

Early assignment of responsibility at home is associated with relatively strong predispositions to prosocial behavior (see p. 98). Temporary assignment of this sort apparently has an analogous and immediate, although perhaps short-lived, effect. For example, some children in the first and second grade met individually with an experimenter who told each child that there was a little girl in the room next door. After a while, the experimenter went out, leaving the child alone. As she left she told each child assigned to the "responsibility condition" that he or she was "in charge" ("if anything happens, you take care of it"). Children in the control group did not receive these instructions. After the experimenter left, a crash was heard, followed by the little girl's sob (actually a tape recording). More of those in the "responsibility" group than in the control group responded to these distress signals and they gave more help. Apparently the assignment of responsibility encouraged the children to act altruistically, perhaps because the experimenter's instructions "disinhibited" their fears of acting this way in new, unfamiliar situations.[47]

Presence of Others

Adults are more likely to show altruism toward others in distress if they are alone rather than with a group of people.[48]

In contrast, in the first and second grades, participating in pairs is more conducive to helping someone in distress than being alone. Among older children (fourth and sixth grades) the trend is somewhat reversed: As much help is given when the children are alone as when they are in pairs. It has been suggested that the presence of another child may reduce younger children's fears and inhibitions and thus increase their prosocial actions, while concern about peers' evaluations may inhibit older children's altruistic reactions. In fact, sixth graders express fear of peer disapproval for inappropriate behavior, and comment that these fears sometimes prevent them from acting altruistically while others are present.[49] Clearly, the presence of others may affect children's predispositions to help; the presence of others appears to enhance this predisposition in younger children but inhibits it in older ones, as it does in adults.

Although we have only sampled some of the many relevant studies, we have been repeatedly impressed with the findings that youngsters modify their prosocial actions as social contexts and environmental situations change. In some cases, an individual's life course may be radically altered by a singular episode or event. Research on situational determinants of prosocial behavior customarily involves experimental manipulation of a salient independent variable (reward, preaching) and subsequent measurement of some form of children's prosocial behavior. Results of such studies indicate that helping, sharing, and donating are enhanced by the following: positive moods, rewards, some types of preaching, certain personality and social characteristics of potential beneficiaries, the presence of peers, and assignment of responsibility for others. Some of these findings—especially those pertaining to rewards, punishments, and preaching—

seem to have obvious pragmatic implications and may be applicable to parental child-rearing and educational practices. Generalizations to natural settings must be regarded as only tentative, however; the validity of inferences and generalizations derived from experimental results must be assessed by direct empirical tests.

Concluding Comments

In the course of this book we have surveyed hundreds of studies. What do the hard data tell us? What do we *know* about the factors controlling the development of prosocial behavior and orientations, and the conditions under which these are manifested? Some conclusions appear to be well-established, confirmed in many studies. Other findings are suggestive rather than definite; some attempts to replicate them have failed. And some studies have yielded contradictory results.

It is appropriate to begin the concluding chapter with a summary of the firm, reliable findings, underscoring some of their implications. Some of these findings enable us to make predictions with confidence; they have clear practical and social implications for programs devised to foster the development of prosocial behavior. Because no single determinant has an overriding influence on prosocial behavior, these predictions apply "in general," with the qualifier "other things being equal." But other things are almost never equal. Each antecedent functions as a part of a complex matrix of factors that exert their influences simultaneously. In this domain, as in other areas of psychology, we cannot predict with certainty the reaction of any particular child in a particular situation. Nevertheless, the predictions are substantially better than chance.

Who are the children who will spontaneously donate some of their own possessions to poor orphans or volunteer to assist classmates who are injured or upset? The data summarized in the chapters on person variables, socialization, and cognitive abilities indicate that they are likely to be relatively self-confident and active children, advanced in moral reasoning as well as in role-taking skills and empathy. Altruists are likely to be the children of nurturant parents who are good models of prosocial behavior, use reasoning in discipline, maintain high standards, and encourage their children to accept responsibilities for others early.

Predictions can also be made about the conditions under which predispositions to prosocial behavior are likely to be translated into action. Children become more helpful when they feel happy or successful; when they receive direct rewards for helping; after they have been exposed to preaching that stresses reasons for helping; if they are assigned responsibility.

The practical value of knowledge of the determinants of prosocial behavior can be demonstrated most forcefully by looking at some possible applications, particularly applications to training procedures. As we have seen, certain parental socialization practices and special training experiences (for example, practice in role-taking and exposure to prosocial models) enhance children's prosocial behavior. Such findings are potentially applicable by many different socializers: parents, educators, clergy, media people. For example, parents who want to raise prosocial children, or to increase the prosocial activities of their children, may be advised, with very little risk, to employ several time-honored practices: modeling helping and sharing behaviors clearly and frequently; reasoning with their children in disciplining them; encouraging the children to reflect on their own and others' feelings, emotions, and expectations; maintaining high standards for the child and being explicit about these; assigning responsibility for others early.

Teachers and religious educators are also frequently in a position to stimulate the development of children's prosocial predispositions, for they, like parents, can reward prosocial behavior when it occurs, serve as models of kindness and generosity, and clarify the feelings and emotions of others in their disciplinary practices. Creative educators can devise role-playing and empathy-promoting class exercises that are exciting to children and, at the same time, increase their prosocial orientations. Conscientious, socially responsible television programming can help raise the levels of helping and sharing among child viewers by decreasing portrayals of violence and aggression and, instead, presenting more instances of exemplary prosocial behavior.

These are only a few examples. Future research will undoubtedly yield other information of social utility. For example, interventions and procedures that advance the level of the child's moral reasoning are being investigated. These include discussions of moral issues, inducing cognitive conflict about moral issues, and role-playing techniques.[1] Preliminary data suggest that these techniques may be effective in raising the levels of moral reasoning. If these initial findings are substantiated, teachers and others can use these techniques to advance children's moral judgments and, thus, strengthen predispositions to prosocial behavior. All applications of this sort should, of course, be guided by research, and the effectiveness of the applicates should be evaluated repeatedly.

As we observed earlier, prosocial behavior is a new research topic. A large proportion of the research we have surveyed was conducted less than ten years ago. Considering this, we think it is remarkable that so much information of social significance and practical utility has been accumulated. But what we have learned so far is only a very small fraction of what we need to know and understand about the genesis and development of prosocial behavior. There are numerous gaps in our knowledge—more unsolved problems than definitive conclusions.

On many occasions in previous chapters, we called attention to deficiencies in our knowledge and understanding of prosocial development. We noted, for example, that almost nothing is known about parental reinforcements of prosocial conduct and their effects on prosocial dispositions. There are as yet no satisfactory answers to questions about the conditions under which high levels of moral reasoning actually lead to prosocial conduct. The possible long-term influences of exposure (especially repeated exposures) to certain "situational determinants," such as good moods or salient preaching, have not been explored adequately. What follows is only a sample of the many additional unsolved problems we regard as important, both theoretically and practically. In our view, none of these problems is insoluble; we will attempt to explicate some future research directions and methods of investigating these critical issues.

Gaps in Theory and Knowledge

Theory plays a key role in guiding research in most scientific disciplines, including psychology and other behavioral sciences. A good theory summarizes and integrates many facts (findings) and explains diverse phenomena in terms of a few broad principles. In addition, theory serves as a source of hypotheses for future research; in this sense it guides research, delineating the next steps to be taken in investigation. The history of science is rich in examples of theories that have generated research breakthroughs or stimulated highly significant investigations. The great strides made in understanding learning are at least partially attributable to the attention given to systematic theory in that area of psychology.

Unfortunately, there is no existing theory that encompasses all aspects of prosocial behavior or integrates even a substantial proportion of the available empirical findings. In this domain, as in many others in the areas of social, developmental, and personality, psychologists are sometimes more challenged by pressing social needs than by theoretical issues. The horror story of Kitty Genovese's murder, in full view of many witnesses (see p. 11), probably set into motion more research on helping and altruism than any theory. Many significant empirical studies of prosocial actions lack a theoretical base.

Construction of comprehensive and meaningful theories of prosocial development must await the accumulation of more substantial and reliable data. At this formative stage of the field, the best we have—and perhaps the most that can be expected—are partial theories, loosely constructed sets of hypotheses, or preliminary conceptual schemata pertaining to *some* antecedents of *some* forms of prosocial behavior. As we have seen, conceptualizations derived from broad systematic psychological theories, such as psychoanalysis, social learning, or cognitive developmental theory, have also been occasional sources of hypotheses about significant determinants.

In addition, there are some stimulating "minitheories," such as Hoffman's, Aronfreed's, and Kohlberg's, each addressed to a critical component of prosocial behavior—Hoffman's and Aronfreed's to the development of empathy and Kohlberg's to the cognitive aspects of morality (see Chapter 8). None of these is a comprehensive theory, and none of them purports to be. Yet each is a source from which hypotheses can be derived, and empirical tests of these hypotheses are likely to lead to further theorizing.

An adequate, comprehensive theory of prosocial development must somehow preserve the natural complexity of the phenomena of prosocial development. Such a theory has to take into account the many and complex determinants as well as the effective interactions among them. Complexity is inherent in this problem and conceptualizations that do not explicitly call attention to this are bound to be inadequate, capable, at best, of explaining only limited parts of the problem.

A first step in the formulation of an integrated theory is a useful and orderly categorization of the dimensions and facts that must be incorporated. One of the main objects of this book is the delineation of critical categories that contain cultural, family socialization, cognitive, and situational variables.

But some other dimensions that are unquestionably of central importance have hardly been investigated at all. There are very few data, for example, on the motivational factors underlying prosocial activities, on the earliest phases of prosocial development, or on the influence of socialization agents outside the home. And, although it is obvious that antecedent variables interact with each other in achieving their effects, there is very little information about these interactions. These are the gaps in knowledge and in theory to which we now turn our attention.

Nonfamilial Socializers

As we have seen, of all the socialization variables affecting prosocial tendencies, parent–child relationships and the mass media have been the most thoroughly examined. But it is readily apparent that other agents of socialization also exert forceful influences. The school situation includes two very important kinds of socializers, teachers and peers who can serve as models and sources of reinforcement; they also preach and nurture. Teachers are, in addition, often in position of assigning responsibility and stimulating the development of their students' role-taking and moral reasoning skills through classroom and recreational activities. It seems reasonable to assume that children will react to their teachers' modeling, preaching, assignment of responsibility for others, and induction as they do to parallel interventions by parents—in direction, if not degree. An admired peer who models helping or reinforces donating may influence the child's subsequent behavior as much as, or more than, a parent.

These are merely inferences, however. Systematic data on the long-term effects of teacher–child and peer–peer interactions on children's prosocial activities are not available. Laboratory and naturalistic research methods could be used appropriately to assess the impacts of special educational techniques in promoting prosocial tendencies, or to explore in depth the conditions under which peers become effective models of helping or sharing. Is the impact made by diverse models cumulative? Are children who have already acquired strong tendencies to help others likely to become even more altruistic as a result of their interactions with peer models? Or is it the child who has very little tendency to behave prosocially who will gain most from contacts with peer or teacher models? Can strong positive influences by socializers outside the home compensate for deficiencies in parental modeling of prosocial behavior?

Motivations and Prosocial Actions

We have observed frequently that decisions regarding prosocial actions are functions of complex interactions of individual and situational variables. It is therefore virtually impossible to predict accurately a particular child's responses across a variety of situations. The motivations underlying prosocial actions are many and varied. Not all helpful acts are altruistic, that is, motivated by the desire to help others; some are instigated by anticipations of reward or social approval.

The problem of the motivations for prosocial behavior is central, although admittedly very complicated, and it is therefore surprising to find how little the problem has been studied. On the basis of theory or speculation, many behavioral scientists have imputed to children motives for helping and sharing (for example, guilt, reduction of empathy-induced feelings of distress, vicarious rewards related to identification, raising self-esteem, gaining approval from others). But, with very few exceptions,[2] investigators have not examined children's motives for prosocial actions directly.

Vitally important information about motivations can be procured by straightforward, skillful interviews of the sort used so effectively by Piaget and others[3] in cognitive developmental research. Children can be asked to explain, in their own terms, why they or others perform acts. Such interviews may be associated with situational tests (for example, questioning a child about why she responded as she did to a cry of distress or to an appeal for donations). A child may be interviewed in naturalistic settings (for example, after assisting a peer who has fallen down on the playground).

Another alternative, the most commonly used one, is to conduct interviews on a more "abstract" level, presenting stories and hypothetical events in which a character has an opportunity to assist another at some self-sacrifice. The child is asked how the situation should be resolved and why the proposed solution is a good one. This technique enables the investigator to examine in depth the child's motivations in a wide range of circumstances. Questions must be asked in flexible ways to insure that the child's own motives—not simply knowledge of the norms of what "should" be done—are freely expressed. The focus must be on the forces that arouse and control children's prosocial tendencies, the factors that instigate helping and generous acts.

Interactions Among Antecedent Variables

Cognitive progress and affective and motivational development are not separate or independent. Advances in cognitive abilities inevitably interact with, and influence, emotional responses, while increased affective maturity undoubtedly has impact on cognitive functions. Cognitive and emotional factors continually interact, governing progress (or regressions) in prosocial tendencies. Yet the consequents of these continued and complicated *interactions* among antecedent variables have been virtually unexplored.

Theories or conceptual schemata in this domain must reflect the "real world," the natural complexities of the problem. Research derived from such conceptualizations would elucidate *interaction effects*, providing information about the conditions under which particular antecedent variables produce their distinctive effects. Situational variables, for example, interact with existing predispositions in influencing the child's reactions to a request for donations or a plea for assistance. It might be predicted that those who have strong, well-established prosocial dispositions are likely to donate to charity or to help others *regardless* of the immediately impinging conditions; those with weaker tendencies toward prosocial action may donate or help only when they are in good moods. Or consider an example of the interaction between socialization experiences and cognitive maturity in regulating prosocial responses. Two sisters whose parents used reasoning as a disciplinary technique attained different levels of moral reasoning. Is the one who is more advanced cognitively more likely than the other to donate to charity or help a peer in need of assistance? Questions of this kind can be answered only by research directly centered on the impact of *interactions* among variables.

While researchers are cognizant of the complicated interrelationships among variables that exert control over prosocial behavior, they typically proceed by examining the effects of one variable at a time. This is probably inevitable in the beginning stages of investigation, and, indeed, this kind of research has proven to be productive. At the same time, the origins and development of helping, sharing, and consideration will not be fully understood until interaction effects are systematically examined through well-designed research. And without basic data on interactions, it is impossible to build meaningful, reality-centered theories of prosocial development.

In-Depth Studies of Altruists

In-depth, multifaceted studies, both naturalistic and clinical, of individuals who have dedicated their lives to work
for humanitarian causes may provide unique opportunities to
probe into the dynamics, motivations, and cognitive operations that direct prosocial actions. These studies, if well designed and properly conducted, may help clarify the intricate
ways in which the many antecedents are interwoven and
interact.

What forces impelled such extraordinary exemplars of
self-sacrifice in behalf of the welfare of others as Mahatma
Gandhi, Albert Schweitzer, Jane Addams, gentiles who
helped Jews escape from the Nazis? It would be fascinating to
assemble detailed biographical information about these
altruists and to use these data to discover their personal motivations and cognitive functioning. Excellent models are
found in the new field of psychohistory, particularly in Erik
Erikson's psychoanalytic and social psychological analyses of
the life and work of Mahatma Gandhi, Martin Luther, and
Thomas Jefferson.[4] Unfortunately, it may be very difficult to
gain access to some of the most essential data, such as objective and reliable evaluations of their personalities and developmental histories. Only very limited generalizations
could be made, but the work would be exciting and most
valuable as a source for generating hypotheses for further,
more rigorous testing.

A fruitful, and more feasible, alternative approach is the
intensive—in part, clinical—study of young adults actively
engaged in humanitarian work. An excellent example of this
approach is Rosenhan's fascinating study of Freedom Riders
(see p. 88). Another is provided by a series of studies in which
Block, Haan, and Smith, investigated the dominant motives

predisposing college students to active concern with broad social issues, such as making personal sacrifices to work for justice and equality for minorities, and to intense involvement in welfare activities (volunteer social service work, hospital work, helping the disadvantaged and handicapped).[5]

In our opinion, the great potential contributions of studies such of these stem from their focus on the individual as a whole—*in vivo,* as it were—and the exploration of the multiple factors operating simultaneously and in complex relationships to each other that direct his or her prosocial orientations and behavior. The kind of clinical and naturalistic study we advocate (depth interviewing; projective, cognitive and other psychological tests; autobiographical writings; reports of early relationships with parents; self-evaluation) permits multidimensional assessment and evaluation of the prosocial consequences of *patterns of interactions* among personal *and* situational variables.

Early Antecedents of Prosocial Orientations

Citing anecdotal reports as support, Hoffman[6] argues that even toddlers under two years of age can exhibit empathy with those in need or distress, which he speculates may be a biologically determined response. This hypothesis may be tenable, but there is no convincing evidence that it is valid. The appearance of empathy early in life has also been explained as a consequence of conditioning, especially within a close mother–child relationship (see p. 128).

The earliest roots of prosocial predispositions have not yet been systematically studied, but recent research on the infant's attachment to its mother seems relevant. Strong early attachment appears to be a major antecedent of early interest in others, and the latter may be a necessary precondition for the development of empathy. Main measured the security of infants' attachments to their mothers at twelve months of age and observed their reactions to an adult playmate, nine months later. Those who had been securely attached to their mothers at the earlier period reacted positively to the play-mate, approaching her readily and playing with her, when they were twenty-one months old. Infants who had been inse-cure in their maternal attachments tended to avoid the play-mate at the later age, generally turning or looking away and refusing to play with her.[7] It may be inferred that strong attachment to the mother in infancy is a precursor of later interest in others and participation in social interactions. Furthermore, children with a strong sense of trust and secu-rity, derived from secure attachments to their mother, are not preoccupied with their own desires and can pay attention to the needs and feelings of others, their "body language," ex-pressions of pleasure or distress, calm or tension.[8]

The child's early-developed empathic capacities can prob-ably be modified by subsequent events. As we have seen, parental use of induction as a disciplinary technique, calling attention to the feelings and emotions of others, probably accentuates the development of empathy; whereas parental insistence on rigid adherence to rules, regardless of the feelings of others probably handicaps such development. Are there sensitive or critical periods in prosocial development? If the child does not develop an adequate capacity for empathy or interest in others early in life—perhaps as a result of insecure attachment to the mother—is he or she likely to have per-manently weak prosocial tendencies? Or can later experiences compensate for early deficiencies in prosocial orientation?

From the very earliest periods of life, the child is continually active, acting *on* the environment, judging and ordering experiences, events, and situations. With increasing age, cognitive abilities become more complex; perceptions, interpretations of environmental events, and judgments become more mature. What effects do these advances in cognitive functions, operating simultaneously with other influences, have on the course of prosocial development? Does more advanced cognitive ability modify, amplify, or mitigate the effects of early influences on prosocial behavior?

In brief, the nature of the early development of prosocial behavior is unknown. Are there discrete, hierarchial qualitatively distinct stages in this development as there are in cognitive development, in moral reasoning, or in life crises? These are key issues for both theory and research, and they could most appropriately be explained in longitudinal investigations.

A Final Word

We close this book with the message with which we began: This is a new domain of study, and there are many more questions than there are definitive answers. To add to the problem, as partial understanding is attained, the issues sometimes seem to become more complicated. This chapter presented a sample of problems that are tasks for future research, but the survey is far from complete; it omits numerous questions yet to be answered. We have pointed out some major gaps in our knowledge of the development of prosocial behavior, choosing, as examples, issues that seem to us to be of looming importance, and we have indicated some possible future directions of research.

The social significance of this field of investigation cannot be overestimated, for it pertains to nothing less than the quality of life, particularly its moral quality. To many of us, the present moral state of humankind already seems deplorable, and it continues to deteriorate. The world seems to be exploding with violence, injustice, inequity, and man's inhumanity to man.

Improvement in the quality of life must begin with changes in the behavior of individuals, specifically greater concern about others, coupled with a willingness to devote considerable effort and energy to promoting the well-being and happiness of others—to insuring that all humans enjoy basic dignity, freedom, rights, and opportunities. It is our thesis that fundamental constructive changes can be effected through the application of knowledge derived from empirical research by psychologists and other behavioral scientists. We have reiterated frequently that such research is hazardous and fraught with difficulties; the results may be disappointing and often discouraging.

But these considerations must be weighed against the potential social benefits to be gained from the application of well-established, reliable research findings, and, in our opinion, these benefits may be incalculable. It would indeed be a sad commentary on psychology and other behavioral sciences if the training and capabilities of experts in these fields, their research skills and creativity, did not prove to be effective in helping to solve urgent social psychological problems.

Betterment of the human condition is one of the distinctive promises of psychology, especially of the fields of developmental and social psychology. The fulfillment of that promise requires intensification and improvement of research on the moral thinking and actions of *individuals*.

NOTES

Chapter 1

1. Turnbull, C. M., *The Mountain People* (New York: Simon and Schuster, 1972).
2. Dennis, W., *The Hopi Child* (New York: Science Editors, Wiley, 1965).
3. Rosenhan, D. L., "Learning Theory and Prosocial Behavior," *Journal of Social Issues,* 28 (1972):151–163.
4. Eisenberg, N. H., "The Development of Prosocial Moral Judgment and Its Correlates" (Ph.D. dissertation, University of California, Berkeley, 1976).

   Ugurel-Semin, R., "Moral Behavior and Moral Judgment of Children," *Journal of Abnormal and Social Psychology,* 42 (1952): 463–474.
5. Goulder, A. W., "The Norm of Reciprocity: A Preliminary Statement," *American Sociological Review,* 125 (1960):161–178.
6. Goranson, R. E. and Berkowitz, L., "Reciprocity and Responsibility Reactions to Prior Help," *Journal of Personality and Social Psychology,* 3 (1966):227–232, *228.**

---

*A final number in italics is the page reference for a direct quotation.

7. Bryan, J. H. and Walbek, N., "Preaching and Practicing Generosity: Children's Action, and Reactions," *Child Development,* 41 (1970):329-353.

8. Staub, E., "Instigation to Goodness: The Role of Social Norms and Interpersonal Influence," *Journal of Social Issues,* 28 (1972):131-150.

9. Kohlberg, L., "Stage and Sequence: The Cognitive-Developmental Approach to Socialization," in *Handbook of Socialization Theory and Research,* ed. D. Goslin (New York: Rand McNally, 1969). Kohlberg, L., "From Is to Ought: How to Commit the Naturalistic Fallacy and Get Away with It in the Study of Moral Development," in *Cognitive Development and Epistemology,* ed. T. Mischel (New York: Academic Press, 1971). Turiel, E., "An Experimental Test of the Sequentiality of Developmental States in the Child's Moral Judgments," *Journal of Personality and Social Psychology,* 3 (1966):611-618. Turiel, E., "Conflict and Transition in Adolescent Moral Development," *Child Development,* 45 (1974):14-29.

10. Hartshorne, H., May, M. A., and Maller, J. B., *Studies in Service and Self Control* (New York: Macmillan, 1929).

Chapter 2

1. Mischel, W., *Introduction to Personality* (Second edition) (New York: Holt, Rinehart and Winston, 1976), p. 149.

2. Hartshorne, H., May, M. A., and Maller, J. B., *Studies in Service and Self Control* (New York: Macmillan, 1929).

3. Murphy, G., Murphy, L. B., and Newcomb, T. M., *Experimental Social Psychology* (Revised edition) (New York: Harper, 1937), p. 622.

4. Burton, R. V., "Generality of Honesty Reconsidered," *Psychological Review,* 70 (1963):481-499.

5. Rutherford, E., and Mussen, P., "Generosity in Nursery School Boys," *Child Development,* 39 (1968):755-765.

6. Friedrich, L. K., and Stein, A. H., "Aggressive and Prosocial Television Programs and the Natural Behavior of Preschool Children," *Monographs of the Society for Research in Child Development,* 38 (1973): Serial No. 151.

7. Yarrow, M. R., and Waxler, C. Z., "Dimensions and Correlates of Prosocial Behavior in Young Children," *Child Development,* 47 (1976):118–125.

8. Block, J., and Block, J. H., *Ego Development and the Provenance of Thought: A Longitudinal Study of Ego and Cognitive Development in Young Children* (progress report for National Institute of Mental Health Grant No. MH16080, January 1973).

9. Rubin, K. H., and Schneider, F. W., "The Relationship Between Moral Judgment, Egocentrism, and Altruistic Behavior," *Child Development,* 44 (1973):661–665.

10. Elliot, R., and Vasta, R., "The Modeling of Sharing: Effects Associated with Vicarious Reinforcement, Symbolization, Age, and Generalization," *Journal of Experimental Child Psychology,* 10 (1970):8–15.

11. Midlarsky, E., and Bryan, J. H., "Affect Expressions and Children's Imitative Altruism," *Journal of Experimental Research in Personality,* 6 (1972):195–203.

12. Krebs, D., and Sturrup, B., "Altruism, Egocentricity, and Behavioral Consistency in Children" (paper presented at the meeting of the American Psychological Association, New Orleans, September 1974).

13. Whiting, B., and Whiting, J. W. M., *Children of Six Cultures* (Cambridge, Mass.: Harvard University Press, 1975).

14. Rushton, J. P. and Wiener, J., "Altruism and Cognitive Development in Children," *British Journal of Social and Clinical Psychology,* 14 (1975):341–349.

15. Dlugokinski, E. L., and Firestone, I. J., "Other Centeredness and Susceptibility to Charitable Appeals: Effects of Perceived Discipline," *Developmental Psychology,* 10 (1974):21–28.

16. Baumrind, D., "Current Patterns of Parental Authority," *Developmental Psychology Monographs,* 1 (1971):1–103.

17. Baumrind, D., personal communication.

18. Bem, D. J., and Allen, A., "On Predicting Some of the People Some of the Time," *Psychological Review* 81 (1974):506–520, *510.*

19. *Ibid.*

20. See, for example, Mussen, P., Rutherford, E., Harris, S., and Keasey, C. B., "Honesty and Altruism Among Preadolescents," *Developmental Psychology,* 3 (1970):169–194; and Staub, E., "Use

of Role Playing and Induction in Training for Prosocial Behavior," *Child Development*, 42 (1971):805–816.

21. Friedrich and Stein, "Aggressive and Prosocial Television"; Krebs and Sturrup, Behavioral Consistency; and Whiting and Whiting, *Children of Six Cultures.*

22. Lindzey, G., "Psychoanalytic Theory and Its Applications in the Social Sciences," in *Handbook of Social Psychology,* ed. G. Lindzey (Cambridge, Mass.: Addison-Wesley, 1954), pp. 153–154.

23. Freud, S., "Group Psychology and the Analysis of the Ego," *The Complete Psychological Works of Sigmund Freud,* Vol. XVIII (London: Hogarth, 1955), p. 121.

24. Glover, E., *The Birth of the Ego* (London: George Allen and Unwin, 1968). Freud, A., *The Ego and Mechanisms of Defense* (London: Hogarth, 1937). Fenichel, O., *The Psychoanalytic Theory of Neurosis* (New York: Norton, 1945).

25. Breger, L., *From Instinct to Identity* (Englewood Cliffs, N. J.: Prentice-Hall, 1973), pp. 256–257.

26. Flugel, J. C., *Man, Morals, and Society* (London: Duckworth and Penguin Books, 1945).

27. Eysenck, H. J., "The Development of Moral Values in Children," *British Journal of Educational Psychology,* 30 (1960):11–21, *13.*

28. Eysenck, H. J., "The Biology of Morality," in *Moral Development and Behavior,* ed. T. Lickona (New York: Holt, Rinehart and Winston, 1976), pp. 108–123, *p. 109.*

29. Hartshorne, May, and Maller, *Studies in Service and Self Control.* Jones, V., "Character Development in Children—An Objective Approach," in *Manual of Child Psychology,* ed. L. Carmichael (New York: Wiley, 1946), pp. 781–832.

30. Maccoby, E. M., "The Development of Moral Values and Behavior in Childhood," in *Socialization and Society,* ed. J. A. Clausen (Boston: Little, Brown, 1968), p. 258.

31. Aronfreed, J., *Conduct and Conscience: The Socialization of Internalized Control Over Behavior* (New York: Academic Press, 1968). Aronfreed, J., "The Socialization of Altruistic and Sympathetic Behavior: Some Theoretical and Experimental Analyses," in

Altruism and Helping Behavior, ed. J. Macauley and L. Berkowitz (New York: Academic Press, 1970).

32. Bandura, A., and Walters, R. H., *Social Learning and Personality Development* (New York: Holt, Rinehart and Winston, 1963).

33. Maccoby, "Moral Values and Behavior," p. 242.

34. Maccoby, "Moral Values and Behavior," p. 242.

35. Kohlberg, quoted by Maccoby, "Moral Values and Behavior," p. 240.

36. Kluckhohn, C., and Murray, H. A. (eds.), *Personality in Nature, Society, and Culture* (New York: Knopf, 1948), p. 59.

37. *Ibid.*

Chapter 3

1. Wilson, E. O., *Sociobiology: The New Synthesis* (Cambridge, Mass.: Harvard University Press, 1975).

2. *Ibid.,* p. 121.

3. *Ibid.,* pp. 3–4.

4. Wilson, E. O., "Human Decency Is Animal," *New York Times Magazine,* October 12, 1975, pp. 38–50, *42.*

5. Trivers, R., "The Evolution of Reciprocal Altruism," *Quarterly Review of Biology,* 46 (1971):35–57.

6. Gould, S. J., "Biological Potential vs. Biological Determinism," *Natural History,* 85(5) (1976):12–22, *20.*

7. Campbell, D. T., "On the Conflicts Between Biological and Social Evolution and Between Psychology and Moral Tradition," *American Psychologist,* 30 (1975):1103–1126.

8. Washburn, S. L., "Biological Versus Social Evolution," *American Psychologist,* 31 (1976):353–355, *354.*

Chapter 4

1. Mead, M., *Sex and Temperament in Three Primitive Societies* (New York: Morrow, 1935), p. 191.

2. Turnbull, C. M., *The Mountain People* (New York: Simon and Schuster, 1972), p. 42.

3. Mead, *Sex and Temperament.*

4. Spiro, M., "Education in a Communal Village in Israel," in *Education and Culture,* ed. G. Spindler (New York: Holt, Rinehart and Winston, 1963), pp. 467–479, *478.*

5. Bronfenbrenner, U., *Two Worlds of Childhood* (New York: Russell Sage Foundation, 1970).

6. Spiro, "Education," p. 479.

7. Campbell, D. T., "The Mutual Methodological Relevance of Anthropology and Psychology," in *Psychological Anthropology,* ed. F. L. K. Hsu (Homewood, Ill.: Dorsey, 1961), pp. 333–352, *334.*

8. Shapira, A., and Madsen, M. C., "Cooperative and Competitive Behavior of Kibbutz and Urban Children in Israel," *Child Development,* 40 (1969):609–617.

9. Madsen, M. C., "Development and Cross-Cultural Differences in the Cooperative and Competitive Behavior of Young Children," *Psychological Reports,* 20 (1967):1307–1320. Madsen, M. C., and Shapira, A., "Cooperative and Competitive Behavior of Urban Afro-American, Anglo-American, Mexican-American, and Mexican-American, and Mexican Village Children," *Developmental Psychology,* 3 (1970):16–20. Madsen, M. C., "Developmental and Cross-Cultural Differences in the Cooperative and Competitive Behavior of Young Children," *Journal of Cross-Cultural Psychology,* 2 (1971):365–371.

10. Shapira and Madsen, "Kibbutz and Urban Children." Shapira, A., and Madsen, M. C., "Between- and Within-Group Cooperation and Competition Among Kibbutz and Nonkibbutz Children," *Developmental Psychology,* 10 (1974):140–145. Shapira, A., and Lomranz, J., "Cooperative and Competitive Behavior of Rural Arab Children in Israel," *Journal of Cross-Cultural Psychology,* 3 (1972):353–359.

11. Marin, G., Mejia, B., and DeOberle, C., "Cooperative as a Function of Place of Residence in Columbian Children," *Journal of Social Psychology,* 95 (1975):127–128.

12. Thomas, D. R., "Cooperation and Competition Among Polynesian and European Children," *Child Development,* 46 (1975):948–953.

13. Marin, Mejia, and DeOberle, "Cooperation." Madsen, "Young Children." Madsen and Shapira, "Mexican Village Children." Miller, A. G., "Integration and Acculturation of Cooperative Behavior Among Blackfoot Indian and Non-Indian Canadian Children," *Journal of Cross-Cultural Psychology*, 4 (1973):374–380. Miller, A. G., and Thomas, R., "Cooperation and Competition Among Blackfoot Indian and Urban Canadian Children," *Child Development*, 43 (1972):1104–1110. Shapira and Madsen, "Kibbutz and Urban Children." Sommerlad, E. A., and Bellingham, W. P., "Cooperation–Competition: A Comparison of Australian and European and Aboriginal School Children," *Journal of Cross-Cultural Psychology*, 3 (1972):149–157.

14. Kagan, S., and Madsen, M. C., "Cooperation and Competition of Mexican, Mexican-American, and Anglo Children of Two Ages," *Developmental Psychology*, 5 (1971):32–39, *38*.

15. Miller and Thomas, "Urban Canadian Children." Miller, "Non-Indian Canadian Children."

16. Madsen, "Young Children," p. 1319.

17. Shapira and Madsen, "Kibbutz and Urban Children," p. 610.

18. Miller and Thomas, "Urban Canadian Children," p. 1105.

19. Kluckhohn, C., "Culture and Behavior," in *Handbook of Social Psychology*, Vol. II, ed. G. Lindzey (Cambridge, Mass.: Addison-Wesley, 1954), pp. 921–976, *p. 961*.

20. Bronfenbrenner, *Two Worlds*.

21. *Ibid.*, p. 21.

22. *Ibid.*, p. 158.

23. Campbell, "Mutual Methodological Relevance," p. 343.

24. Whiting, J. W. M., and Whiting, B. B., "Altruistic and Egoistic Behavior in Six Cultures," in *Cultural Illness and Health*, ed. L. Nader and T. W. Maretzki (Washington, D.C.: American Anthropological Association, 1973), pp. 56–66. Whiting, B. B., and Whiting, J. W. M., *Children of Six Cultures: A Psychocultural Analysis* (Cambridge, Mass.: Harvard University Press, 1975).

25. Whiting and Whiting, "Behavior in Six Cultures," p. 64.

26. Whiting and Whiting, "Behavior in Six Cultures," p. 63.

27. Bronfenbrenner, *Two Worlds*.

Chapter 5

1. DePalma, D. J., "Effects of Social Class, Moral Orientation and Severity of Punishment on Boys' Moral Responses to Transgression and Generosity," *Developmental Psychology,* 10 (1974):890–900. Friedrich, L. K. and Stein, A. H., "Aggressive and Prosocial Television Programs and The Natural Behavior of Preschool Children," *Monographs of the Society for Research in Child Development.* 38 (1973): Serial No. 151. Madsen, M. C., "Developmental and Cross-Cultural Differences in the Cooperative and Competitive Behavior of Young Children," *Journal of Cross-Cultural Psychology,* 2 (1971):365–371.

2. Berkowitz, L., "Responsibility, Reciprocity, and Social Distance in Help Giving," *Journal of Experimental Social Psychology,* 4 (1968):46–63.

3. Dreman, S. B., and Greenbaum, C. W., "Altruism or Reciprocity: Sharing Behavior in Israeli Kindergarten Children," *Child Development,* 44 (1973):61–68. Dreman, S. B., "Sharing Behavior in Israeli Children: Cognitive and Social Learning Factors," *Child Development,* 47 (1976):186–194. Berkowitz and Freedman, "Social Class Differences."

4. Hartup, W. W., and Keller, E. D., "Nurturance in Preschool Children and Its Relation to Dependency," *Child Development,* 31 (1960):681–689. Presbie, R. J., and Kanereff, V. T., "Sharing in Children as a Function of the Number of Sharees and Reciprocity," *Journal of Genetic Psychology,* 116 (1970):31–44. Yarrow, M. R., and Waxler, C. Z., "Dimensions and Correlates of Prosocial Behavior in Young Children," *Child Development,* 47 (1976):118–125.

5. Barnett, M. A., and Bryan, J. H., "Effects of Competition With Outcome Feedback on Children's Helping Behavior," *Developmental Psychology,* 10 (1974):838–842. Elliot, R., and Vasta, R., "The Modeling of Sharing: Effects Associated With Vicarious Reinforcement, Symbolization, Age, and Generalization," *Journal of Empirical and Child Psychology,* 10 (1970):8–15. Emler, N. P., and Rushton, J. P., "Cognitive-Developmental Factors in Children's Generosity," *British Journal of Social and Clinical Psychology,* 13 (1974):277–281. Green, F. P., and Schneider, F. W., "Age Differences in the Behavior of Boys on Three Measures of

Altruism," *Child Development*, 45 (1974):248–251. Hanlon, B. J., and Gross, P., "The Development of Sharing Behavior," *Journal of Abnormal and Social Psychology*, 59 (1959):425–428. Gelfand, D. M., Hartmann, D. P., Cromer, C. C., Smith, C. L., and Page, B. C., "The Effects of Instructional Prompts and Praise on Children's Donation Rates," *Child Development*, 46 (1975): 980–983. Harris, M. B., "Models, Norms, and Sharing," *Psychological Reports*, 29 (1971):147–153. Iannotti, R. J., The Effects of Role Taking Experiences on Role Taking, Altruism, Empathy, and Aggression (paper presented at the biennial meeting of the Society for Research in Child Development, Denver, April 1975). Maruyamma, G., Jackson-White, R., Fraser, S. C., Beasman, A. L., Chong, E., Gutowski, J., Thompson, W., and Wong, K. (paper presented at the Western Psychological Association, Sacramento, April 1975). Midlarsky, E., and Bryan, J. H., "Affect Expressions and Children's Imitative Altruism," *Journal of Experimental Research in Personality*, 6 (1972):195–203. Moore, T., and Ucko, L. W., "Four to Six: Constructiveness and Conflict in Meeting Doll Play Problems," *Journal of Child Psychology and Psychiatry*, 2 (1961):21–47. Moore, B. S., Underwood, B., and Rosenhan, D. L., "Affect and Altruism," *Developmental Psychology*, 8 (1973):99–104. Rushton, J. P., and Weiner, J., "Altruism and Cognitive Development in Children," *British Journal of Social and Clinical Psychology*, 14 (1975):341–349. Ugur-el-Semin, R., "Moral Behavior and Moral Judgment of Children," *Journal of Abnormal and Social Psychology*, 47 (1952):463–474. White, G. M., and Burnam, M. A., "Socially Cued Altruism: Effects of Modeling Instructions and Age on Public and Private Donations," *Child Development*, 46 (1975):559–563. Whiting, B. B., and Whiting, J. W. M., *Children of Six Cultures: A Psychocultural Analysis* (Cambridge, Mass.: Harvard University Press, 1975).

6. Emler and Rushton, "Cognitive-Developmental Factors." Friedrich and Stein, "Aggressive and Prosocial Television." Harris, M. B., "Reciprocity and Generosity: Some Determinants of Sharing In Children," *Child Development*, 41 (1970):313–328. Harris, "Models, Norms, and Sharing." Isen, A. M., Horn, N., and Rosenhan, D. L., "Effects of Success and Failure on Children's Generosity," *Journal of Personality and Social Psychology*, 27

(1973):239–247. Krebs, D. L., "Altruism: An Examination of the Concept and a Review of the Literature," *Psychological Bulletin,* 73 (1970):258–302. O'Bryant, S. L., and Brophy, J. E., "Sex Differences in Altruistic Behavior," *Developmental Psychology,* 12 (1976):554. Olejnik, A. B., Developmental Changes and Interrelationships Among Role-Taking Moral Judgments and Children's Sharing (paper presented at The Biennial Meeting of the Society for Research in Child Development, Denver, April 1975). Olejnik, A. B., and McKinney, J. P., "Parental Value Orientation and Generosity in Children," *Developmental Psychology,* 8 (1973):311. Rubin, K. H., and Schneider, F. W., "The Relationship Between Moral Judgment, Egocentrism, and Altruistic Behavior," *Child Development,* 44 (1973):661–665. Staub, E., "Helping a Person in Distress: The Influence of Implicit and Explicit 'Rules' of Conduct on Children and Adults," *Journal of Personality and Social Psychology,* 17 (1971):137–144. Yarrow and Waxler, "Dimensions and Correlates."

7. Harris, M. B., and Siebel, C. E., "Affect, Aggression, and Altruism," *Developmental Psychology,* 11 (1975):623–627. Hoffman, M. L., "Developmental Synthesis of Affect and Cognition and Its Implications for Altruistic Motivation," *Developmental Psychology,* 11 (1975):607–622. Midlarsky and Bryan, "Children's Imitative Altruism." Moore et al., "Affect and Altruism." Rice, M. E., and Grusec, J. E., "Saying and Doing Effects of Observer Performance," *Journal of Personality and Social Psychology,* 32 (1975):584–593. White, G. M., "Immediate and Deferred Effects of Model Observation and Guided and Unguided Rehearsal on Donating and Stealing," *Journal of Personality and Social Psychology,* 21 (1972):139–148. Whiting and Whiting, *Children of Six Cultures.*

8. Hoffman, M. L., and Levine, L. E., "Early Sex Differences In Empathy," *Developmental Psychology,* 12 (1976):557–558.

9. Gelfand et al., "Children's Donation Rates." Dreman and Greenbaum, "Altruism or Reciprocity." Handlon and Gross, "Sharing Behavior."

10. Ribal, J. E., "Social Character and Meaning of Selfishness and Altruism," *Sociology and Social Research,* 47 (1963):311–321. Sawyer, J., "The Altruism Scale: A Measure of Cooperative,

Individualistic and Competitive Interpersonal Orientation," *American Journal of Sociology,* 71 (1966):407–416. Ugurel-Semin, "Moral Behavior."

11. Staub, E., "A Child in Distress: The Influence of Nurturance and Modeling on Children's Attempts to Help," *Developmental Psychology,* 5 (1971):124–132. Staub, E., "Use of Role Playing and Induction in Training for Prosocial Behavior," *Child Development,* 42 (1971):805–816.

12. Staub, "A Child in Distress." Staub, "Use of Role Playing."

13. Whiting and Whiting, *Children of Six Cultures.*

14. Rutherford, E., and Mussen, P., "Generosity in Nursery School Boys," *Child Development,* 39 (1968):755–765.

15. Lenrow, P. B., "Studies in Sympathy," in *Affect, Cognition, and Personality: Empirical Studies,* ed. S. S. Tomkins and C. E. Izard (New York: Springer, 1965), pp. 264–294.

16. Hartup and Keller, "Nurturance in Preschool Children."

17. Staub, "A Child in Distress."

18. Murphy, L. B., *Social Behavior and Child Personality* (New York: Columbia University Press, 1937).

19. Friedrich and Stein, "Aggressive and Prosocial Television."

20. Yarrow and Waxler, "Dimensions and Correlates."

21. Bryan, J. H., "Children's Cooperation and Helping Behaviors," in *Review of Child Development Research,* Vol. 5, ed. E. M. Hetherington (Chicago: University of Chicago Press, 1975), pp. 127–180.

22. Block, J., and Block, J. H., "Ego Development and the Provenance of Thought: A Longitudinal Study of Ego and Cognitive Development in Young Children" (progress report to the National Institute of Mental Health, Grant No. MH16080, January 1973).

23. Long, G. T., and Lerner, M. J., "Deserving, the 'Personal Contact,' and Altruistic Behavior by Children," *Journal of Personality and Social Psychology,* 29 (1974):551–556.

24. Bond, N. D., and Philips, B. N., "Personality Traits Associated with Altruistic Behavior of Children," *Journal of School Psychology,* 9 (1) (1971):24–34.

25. Mussen, P., Rutherford, E., Harris, S., and Keasey, C. B., "Honesty and Altruism Among Preadolescents," *Developmental Psychology,* 3 (1970):169–194.
26. Staub, E., "A Child in Distress: The Effects of Focusing Responsibility on Children on Their Attempts to Help," *Developmental Psychology,* 2 (1970):152–153.
27. Midlarsky and Bryan, "Children's Imitative Altruism."
28. Pomazal, R. J., and Jaccard, J. J., "An Informational Approach to Altruistic Behavior," *Journal of Personality and Social Psychology,* 33 (1976):317–326. Staub, E., "Helping a Distressed Person: Social, Personality, and Stimulus Determinants," in *Advances in Experimental Social Psychology,* Vol. 7, ed. L. Berkowitz (New York: Academic Press, 1974). Trimakas, K. A., and Nicolay, R. C., "Self Concept and Altruism in Old Age," *Journal of Gerontology,* 29 (4) (1974):434–439. Wilson, J. P., "Motivation, Modeling and Altruism: A Person X Situation Analysis," *Journal of Personality and Social Psychology,* 34 (1976):1078–1086.

Chapter 6

1. Block, J., "Q-Sort: Child Rearing Attitudes" (unpublished manuscript, University of California, Berkeley, 1969).
2. Midlarsky, E., Bryan, J. H., and Brickman, P. "Aversive Approval: Interactive Effects of Modeling and Reinforcement on Altruistic Behavior," *Child Development,* 44 (1973):321–328. Harris, M. B., "Reciprocity and Generosity: Some Determinants of Sharing in Children," *Child Development,* 41 (1970):313–328. Harris, M. B., "Models, Norms, and Sharing," *Psychological Reports,* 29 (1971):147–153. White, G. M., and Burnam, M. A., "Socially Cued Altruism Effects of Modeling Instructions and Age on Public and Private Donations," *Child Development,* 46 (1975):559–563.
3. Rosenhan, D., "Some Origins of Concern for Others," in *Trends and Issues in Developmental Psychology,* ed. P. Mussen, J. Langer, and M. Covington (New York: Holt, Rinehart and Winston, 1969), pp. 134–153.

4. Rushton, J. P., "Generosity in Children: Immediate and Long Term Effects of Modeling, Preaching, and Moral Judgment," *Journal of Personality and Social Psychology,* 31 (1975):3, 459–466. Rice, M. E., and Grusec, J. E., "Saying and Doing: Effects of Observer Performance," *Journal of Personality and Social Psychology,* 32 (1975):584–593.

5. Elliot, R., and Vasta, R., "The Modeling of Sharing: Effects Associated with Vicarious reinforcement, Symbolization, Age, and Generalization," *Journal of Experimental Child Psychology,* 10 (1970):8–15.

6. Midlarsky, E., and Bryan, J. H. "Affect Expressions and Children's Imitative Altruism," *Journal of Experimental Research in Personality,* 6 (1972):195–203.

7. Rushton, "Generosity in Children."

8. Rushton, J. P., "Socialization and the Altruistic Behavior of Children," *Psychological Bulletin,* 83 (1976):898–913.

9. Grusec, J. E., "Power and the Internalization of Self Denial," *Child Development,* 42 (1971):93–105.

10. Bryan, J. H., and Walbek, N., "Preaching and Practicing Generosity: Children's Action, and Reactions," *Child Development,* 41 (1970):329–353.

11. Bryan, J. H., "Children's Cooperation and Helping Behaviors," in *Review of Child Development Research,* Vol. 5, ed. E. M. Hetherington (Chicago: University of Chicago Press, 1975), pp. 127–180.

12. Grusec, J. E., and Skubinski, S. L., "Model Nurturance, Demand Characteristics of the Modeling Experiment, and Altruism," *Journal of Personality and Social Psychology,* 14 (1970): 352–359. Rosenhan, D., and White, G. M., "Observation and Rehearsal as Determinants of Prosocial Behavior," *Journal of Personality and Social Psychology,* 5 (1967):424–431. Grusec, "Self Denial." Weissbrod, C. S., "The Effect of Noncontingent Adult Warmth on Reflective and Impulsive Children's Donation and Rescue Behavior" (paper presented at the Annual Meeting of the Midwest Psychological Association, Chicago, 1974).

13. Staub, E., "A Child in Distress: The Influence of Nurturance and Modeling on Children's Attempts to Help," *Developmental*

Psychology, 5 (1971):124–132. Weissbrod, Non-contingent Adult Warmth.

14. Bryan, "Children's Cooperation," p. 149.
15. Staub, "A Child in Distress," p. 130.
16. Yarrow, M. R., Scott, P., and Waxler, C. Z., "Learning Concern for Others," *Developmental Psychology,* 8 (1973):240–260.
17. *Ibid.,* p. 246.
18. *Ibid.,* p. 251.
19. *Ibid.,* p. 253.
20. *Ibid.,* p. 256.
21. Rutherford, E., and Mussen, P., "Generosity in Nursery School Boys," *Child Development,* 39 (1968):755–765.
22. Hoffman, M. L., "Altruistic Behavior and the Parent-Child Relationship," *Journal of Personality and Social Psychology,* 31 (1975):937–943.
23. London, P., "The Rescuers: Motivational Hypotheses About Christians Who Saved Jews from the Nazis," in *Altruism and Helping Behavior,* ed. J. Macaulay and L. Berkowitz (New York: Academic Press, 1970), pp. 241–250.
24. Rosenhan, "Concern for Others."
25. Rosenhan, D., "Prosocial Behavior of Children," in *The Young Child: Reviews of Research,* Vol. 2, ed. W. W. Hartup (Washington, D.C.: National Association for the Education of Young Children, 1972), pp. 340–359, *342.*
26. Rutherford and Mussen, "Generosity."
27. Yarrow, M. R., and Scott, R. M., "Imitation of Nurturant and Non-nurturant Models," *Journal of Personality and Social Psychology,* 23 (1972):259–270.
28. Hoffman, M., and Saltzstein, H. D., "Parent Discipline, and the Child's Moral Development," *Journal of Personality and Social Psychology,* 5 (1967):45–57.
29. Feshbach, N., "The Relationship of Child Rearing Factors to Children's Aggression, Empathy, and Related Positive and Negative Social Behaviors" (paper presented at the NATO Conference on the Determinants and Origins of Aggressive Behavior, Monte Carlo, Monaco, July 1973).

30. Hoffman, "Altruistic Behavior."
31. Hoffman, M., "Parent Discipline and the Child's Consideration of Others," *Child Development*, 34 (1963):573–588. Hoffman and Saltzstein, "Child's Moral Development."
32. Hoffman and Saltzstein, "Child's Moral Development," p. 553.
33. *Ibid.*, p. 558.
34. *Ibid.*, p. 558.
35. Hoffman, "Child's Consideration of Others."
36. Dlugokinski, E., and Firestone, I. J., "Other Centeredness and Susceptibility to Charitable Appeals: Effects of Perceived Discipline," *Developmental Psychology*, 10 (1974):21–28.
37. Feshbach, Child Rearing Factors.
38. Hoffman, "Child's Consideration of Others."
39. Baumrind, D., "Current Patterns of Parental Authority," *Developmental Psychology Monographs*, 1 (1971):1–103.
40. Whiting, B., and Whiting, J. W. M., *Children of Six Cultures* (Cambridge, Mass.: Harvard University Press, 1975).
41. Staub, E., and Jancaterino, W., Teaching Others, Participation in Prosocial Action and Prosocial Induction as a Means of Children Learning to be Helpful (research cited in "To Rear A Prosocial Child," in *Moral Development, Current Theory and Research*, ed. D. J. DePalma and J. M. Foley; Hillsdale, N. J.: Lawrence Erlbaum, 1975).

Chapter 7

1. See, for example, Bandura, A., *Principles of Behavior Modification* (New York: Holt, Rinehart and Winston, 1969).
2. Bryan, J. H., and Walbek, N., "Preaching and Practicing Generosity: Children's Action, and Reactions," *Child Development*, 41 (1970):329–353. Bryan, J. H., and Walbek, N., "The Impact of Words and Deeds Concerning Altruism Upon Children," *Child Development*, 41 (1970):747–759. Elliot, R., and Vasta, R., "The Modeling of Sharing: Effects Associated with Vicarious Reinforcement, Symbolization, Age, and Generalization," *Journal of*

Experimental Child Psychology, 10 (1970):8–15. Hartup, W. W., and Coates, B., "Imitation of a Peer as a Function of Reinforcement From the Peer Group and Rewardingness of the Model," *Child Development,* 38 (1967):1003–1016. Liebert, R. M., Fernandez, L. E., and Gill, L., "Effects of a 'Friendless' Model on Imitation and Prosocial Behavior," *Psychonomic Science,* 16 (1969):81–82.

3. Johnson, M., quoted in Liebert, R. M., Neale, J. M., and Davidson, E. S., *The Early Window: Effects of Television on Children and Youth* (New York: Pergamon, 1973), p. 170.

4. Liebert, R. M., Neale, J. M., and Davidson, E. S., *The Early Window: Effects of Television on Children and Youth* (New York: Pergamon 1973), p. 170.

5. See, for example, Rubenstein, E. A., Comstock, G. A., and Murray, J. P. (eds.), *Television and Social Behavior,* Vols. 1–5 (Washington, D.C.: Government Printing Office, 1972).

6. Eron, L. D., Lefkowitz, M. M., Huesmann, L. R., and Walder, L. O., "Does Television Violence Cause Aggression?" *American Psychologist,* 27 (1972):253–263.

7. Hapkiewitz, W. G., and Roden, A. H., "The Effects of Aggressive Cartoons on Children's Interpersonal Play," *Child Development,* 42 (1971):1583–1585. Stein, A. H., Friederich, L. K., Deutsch, F., and Nydegger, C., The Effects of Aggressive Prosocial Television on Social Interaction of Preschool Children (paper presented at the meeting of the Midwestern Psychological Association, Chicago, May 1973).

8. Coates, B., Pusser, H. E., and Goodman, I., "The Influence of 'Sesame Street' and 'Mister Rogers' Neighborhood' on Children's Social Behavior in Preschool," *Child Development,* 47 (1976):1, 138–144. Friedrich, L. K., and Stein, A. H., "Aggressive and Prosocial Television Programs and the Natural Behavior of Preschool Children," *Monographs of the Society for Research in Child Development,* 38 (1973): Serial No. 151. Friedrich, L. K., and Stein, A. H., "Prosocial Television and Young Children: The Effects of Verbal Labeling and Role Playing on Learning and Behavior," *Child Development,* 46 (1975):27–38. Paulson, F. L., "Teaching Cooperation on Television: An Evaluation of

Sesame Street Social Goals Program," A. V. Communication Review, 22 (1974):220–246. Shirley, K. W., "The Prosocial Effects of Publicly Broadcast Children's Television" (Ph.D. dissertation, University of Kansas, 1974). Cosgrove, M., and McIntyre, C. W., "The Influence of 'Misterogers' Neighborhood' on Nursery School Children's Prosocial Behavior" (paper presented at the meeting of the Southeastern Regional Society for Research in Child Development, Chapel Hill, N.C., March 1974).

9. Friedrich and Stein, "Aggressive and Prosocial Television." Friedrich and Stein, "Prosocial Television and Young Children."

10. Friederich and Stein, "Aggressive and Prosocial Television."

11. Friedrich and Stein, "Prosocial Television and Young Children," p. 37.

12. Coates et al., "Children's Social Behavior in Preschool."

13. Sprafkin, J. N., Liebert, R. M., and Poulos, R. W., "Effects of a Prosocial Televised Example on Children's Helping," *Journal of Experimental Child Psychology*, 20 (1975):119–126.

14. Bryan and Walbek, "The Impact of Words and Deeds." Elliot and Vasta, "The Modeling of Sharing." Rushton, J. P., and Owen, D., "Immediate and Delayed Effects of TV Modeling and Preaching on Children's Generosity," *British Journal of Social and Clinical Psychology*, 14 (1975):309–310.

15. Liebert, Neale, and Davidson, *The Early Window*, p. 109.

16. Liebert, Neale, and Davidson, *The Early Window*, p. 171.

Chapter 8

1. Krebs, D., and Sturrup, B., "Altruism, Egocentricity, and Behavioral Consistency in Children" (paper presented at the meeting of the American Psychological Association, New Orleans, September 1974).

2. Mussen, P., Rutherford, E., Harris, S., and Keasey, C. B., "Honesty and Altruism Among Preadolescents," *Developmental Psychology*, 3 (1970):169–194.

3. Hansen, R., Goldman, B. D., and Baldwin, M., Towards a Taxonomy of Altruism: An Observational Study of Spontaneous Prosocial Behavior Among Young Children (paper presented at the annual meeting of the Canadian Psychological Association, Quebec City, Province of Quebec, Canada, June 1975). Hartshorne, H., May, M. A., and Maller, J. B., *Studies in Service and Self Control* (New York: Macmillan, 1929). Rubin, K. H., and Schneider, F. W., "The Relationship Between Moral Judgment, Egocentrism, and Altruistic Behavior," *Child Development,* 44 (1973):661–665. Rushton, J. P., and Wiener, J., "Altruism and Cognitive Development in Children," *British Journal of Social and Clinical Psychology,* 14 (1975): 341–349. Friedrich, L. K., and Stein, A. H., "Aggressive and Prosocial Television Programs and the Natural Behavior of Preschool Children," *Monographs of the Society for Research in Child Development,* 38 (1973): Serial No. 151.

4. Kohlberg, L., "From Is to Ought: How to Commit the Naturalistic Fallacy and Get Away With It in the Study of Moral Development," in *Cognitive Development and Epistemology,* ed. T. Mischel (New York: Academic Press, 1971), p. 228.

5. Vidal, G., *Burr* (New York: Random House, 1973). Quoted in *Moral Development and Behavior,* ed. T. Lickona (New York: Holt, Rinehart and Winston, 1976), p. 202.

6. Piaget, J., *The Moral Judgment of the Child* (Glencoe, Ill.: Free Press, 1948).

7. *Ibid.,* p. 106.

8. Abel, T., "Moral Judgments Among Subnormals," *Journal of Abnormal Psychology,* 36 (1941):378–392. Bandura, A., and McDonald, F. J., "Influence of Social Reinforcement and the Behavior of Models in Shaping Children's Moral Judgments," *Journal of Abnormal and Social Psychology,* 67 (1963):274–281. Cowan, P. A., Langer, J., Heavenrich, J., and Nathanson, M., "Social Learning and Piaget's Cognitive Theory of Moral Development," *Journal of Personality and Social Psychology,* 11 (1969):261–274. Grinder, R. E., "Relations Between Behavioral and Cognitive Dimensions of Conscience in Middle Childhood," *Child Development,* 35 (1964):881–891. Harrower, M. R., "Social Status and Moral Development of the Child,"

British Journal of Educational Psychology, 4 (1934):75-95. Jahoda, G., "Immanent Justice Among West African Children," *Journal of Social Psychology,* 47 (1958):241-248. Johnson, R. C., "A Study of Children's Moral Judgments," *Child Development,* 33 (1962):327-354. Lerner, E., *Constraint Areas and Moral Judgment of Children* (Menasha, Wis.: Banta, 1937). Lerner, E., "The Problem of Perspective in Moral Reasoning," *American Journal of Sociology,* 43 (1937):247-269. Liu, C. H., "The Influence of Cultural Background on Moral Judgment of Children" (Ph.D. dissertation, Columbia University, 1950). MacRae, D., Jr., "A Test of Piaget's Theories of Moral Development," *Journal of Abnormal and Social Psychology,* 49 (1954):195-206. Magowan, S. A., and Lee, T., "Some Sources of Error in the Use of the Projective Method for the Measurement of Moral Judgment," *British Journal of Psychology,* 61 (1970):535-543. Medinnus, G. R., "Objective Responsibility in Children: A Comparison with the Piaget Data," *Journal of Genetic Psychology,* 191 (1962):127-133. Stuart, R. B., "Decentration in the Development of Children's Concepts of Moral and Causal Judgment," *Journal of Genetic Psychology,* 111 (1967):59-68. Whiteman, P. H., and Kosier, P., "Development of Children's Moralistic Judgments: Age, Sex, IQ, and Certain Personal Experiential Variables, *Child Development,* 35 (1964):843-851.

9. Kohlberg, L., "The Development of Children's Orientations Toward a Moral Order: Sequence in the Development of Moral Thought,"*Vita Humana,* 6 (1963):11-33. Kohlberg, L., "Development of Moral Character and Ideology," in *Review of Child Development Research,* Vol. 1, ed. M. L. Hoffman and L. W. Hoffman (New York: Russell Sage Foundation, 1964). Kohlbert, "From Is to Ought."

10. Kohlberg, L., "Stage and Sequence: The Cognitive-Developmental Approach to Socialization," in *Handbook of Socialization Theory and Research,* ed. D. Goslin (New York: Rand McNally, 1969). White, C., "Moral Development in Bahamian School Children: A Cross Cultural Examination of Kohlberg's Stages of Moral Reasoning," *Developmental Psychology,* 11 (1975):535-536. Gorsuch, R. L., and Barnes, M. L., "Stages of Ethical Reasoning and Moral Norms of Caribbean Youths," *Journal of Cross-Cultural Psychology,* 4 (1973):283-301.

11. Lee, L. C., "The Concomitant Development of Cognitive and Moral Modes of Thought: A Test of Selected Deductions From Piaget's Theory," *Genetic Psychology Monographs,* 83 (1971):93–143. Kuhn, D., Langer, J., Kohlberg, L., and Haan, N., "The Development of Formal Operations in Logical and Moral Judgment," *Genetic Psychology Monographs,* in press. Harris, S., Mussen, P., and Rutherford, E., "Some Cognitive, Behavioral, and Personality Correlates of Maturity of Moral Judgment," *Journal of Genetic Psychology,* 128 (1976):123–135. Arbuthnot, J., "Relationships Between Maturity of Moral Judgment and Measures of Cognitive Abilities," *Psychological Reports,* 33 (1973):945–946. Thomlinson-Keasey, C., and Keasey, C. B., "The Mediating Role of Cognitive Development in Moral Judgment," *Child Development,* 45 (1974):291–298

12. Selman, R., "The Relation of Role Taking to the Development of Moral Judgment in Children," *Child Development,* 42 (1971):79–91. Giraldo, M., "Moral Development and its Relation to Role Taking Ability and Interpersonal Behavior" (Ph.D. dissertation, Catholic University of America, 1972). Ambron, S. R., and Irwin, D. M., "Role Taking and Moral Judgment in Five and Seven Year Olds," *Developmental Psychology,* 11 (1975):102. Moir, D. J., "Egocentrism and the Emergence of Conventional Morality in Preadolescent Girls," *Child Development,* 45 (1974):299–309. Olejnik, A. B., Developmental Changes and Interrelationships Among Role-Taking, Moral Judgments and Children's Sharing (paper presented at the biennial meeting of the Society for Research in Child Development, Denver, April 1975). Rubin and Schneider, "Altruistic Behavior."

13. Eisenberg, N. H., "The Development of Prosocial Moral Judgment and Its Correlates" (Ph.D. dissertation, University of California, Berkeley, 1976).

14. Kohlberg, "Stage and Sequence."

15. Eisenberg, "Prosocial Moral Judgment."

16. Kohlberg, "Children's Orientations." Krebs, R. L., "Some Relationships Between Moral Judgment, Attention, and Resistance to Temptation" (Ph.D. dissertation, University of Chicago, 1968). Nelson, E. A., Grinder, R. E., and Biaggio, A. M.,

"Relationships Among Behavioral, Cognitive Development, and Self Report Measures of Morality and Personality," *Multivariate Behavioral Research*, 4 (1969):483–500. Schwartz, W., Feldman, K., Brown, M., and Heingartner, H., "Some Personality Correlates of Conduct in Two Situations of Moral Conflict," *Journal of Personality*, 37 (1969):41–57.

17. Kohlberg, "Stage and Sequence." Rubin and Schneider, "Altruistic Behavior." Rushton and Wiener, "Altruism and Cognitive Development." Staub, E., "Helping a Distressed Person: Social, Personality, and Stimulus Determinants," in *Advances in Experimental Social Psychology*, Vol. 7, ed. L. Berkowitz (New York: Academic Press, 1974). Eisenberg, "Prosocial Moral Judgment."

18. Emler, N. P., and Rushton, J. P., "Cognitive-Developmental Factors in Children's Generosity," *British Journal of Social and Clinical Psychology*, 13 (1974):277–281, *277*.

19. Olejnik, Developmental Changes.

20. McNamee, S. M., "Moral Behavior, Moral Development, and Needs in Students and Political Activists, With Special Reference to the Law and Order Stage of Development" (Ph.D. dissertation, Case Western Reserve University, Cleveland, 1972).

21. Rubin and Schneider, "Altruistic Behavior."

22. Harris, Mussen, and Rutherford, "Maturity of Moral Judgment."

23. Feshbach, N. D., Empathy in Children: A Special Ingredient of Social Development (paper given at the Western Psychological Association meetings, Los Angeles, April 1976), p. 2. See also: Feshbach, N. D., "The Relationship of Child Rearing Factors to Children's Aggression, Empathy, and Related Positive and Negative Social Behaviors," in *Determinants and Origins of Aggressive Behavior*, ed. J. De Wit and W. W. Hartup (The Hague, Neth.: Mouton, 1975), pp. 427–436, and Feshbach, N. D., "Studies on the Empathic Behavior on Children," in *Progress in Experimental Personality Research*, Vol. 8, ed. B. A. Maher (New York: Academic Press, 1977).

24. Feshbach, "Empathy in Children," p. 3

25. Flavell, J., *The Development of Role Taking and Communication Skills in Children* (New York: Wiley, 1968).

26. Fay, B. M., "The Relationship of Cognitive Moral Judgment, Generosity, and Empathic Behavior in Six- and Eight-Year-Old Children" (Ph.D. dissertation, University of California, Los Angeles, 1970), Feshbach, N., and Roe, L., "Empathy in Six- and Seven-Year-Olds," *Child Development,* 39 (1968):133–145.

27. Aronfreed, J., *Conduct and Conscience: The Socialization of Internalized Control Over Behavior* (New York: Academic Press, 1968). Aronfreed, J., "The Socialization of Altruistic and Sympathetic Behavior: Some Theoretical and Experimental Analyses," in *Altruism and Helping Behavior,* ed. J. Macauley and L. Berkowitz (New York: Academic Press, 1970), pp. 103–126. Hoffman, M. L., "Developmental Synthesis of Affect and Cognition and its Implications for Altruistic Motivation," *Developmental Psychology,* 11 (1975):607–622. Hoffman, M. L., "Empathy, Role-taking, Guilt, and Development of Altruistic Motives," in *Moral Development and Behavior,* ed. T. Lickona (New York: Holt, Rinehart and Winston 1976), pp. 124–143.

28. Aronfreed, *Conduct and Conscience.* Aronfreed, "Altruistic and Sympathetic Behavior."

29. Ekstein, R., "Psychoanalysis and Education for the Facilitation of Positive Human Qualities," *Journal of Social Issues,* 28 (1972):71–86. Olden, C., "Notes on the Development of Empathy," *The Psychoanalytic Study of the Child,* 13 (1958):505–518. Sullivan, H. S., *Conceptions of Modern Psychiatry* (New York: Norton, 1940).

30. Wright, D., *The Psychology of Moral Behavior* (Middlesex, Eng.: Penguin Books, 1971), p. 135.

31. Hoffman, "Altruistic Motivation."

32. Hoffman, "Altruistic Motivation," p. 610.

33. Hoffman, "Altruistic Motivation," p. 613.

34. Hoffman, "Altruistic Motivation," p. 615.

35. Hoffman, "Altruistic Motivation," p. 616.

36. Hoffman, "Altruistic Motivation," p. 617.

37. Borke, H., "Interpersonal Perception of Young Children: Egocentricity or Empathy?" *Developmental Psychology,* 5 (1971):

263–269.

38. Iannotti, R. J., The Many Faces of Empathy: An Analysis of the Definition and Evaluation of Empathy in Children (paper presented at the biennial meeting of the Society for Research in Child Development, Denver, April 1975).

39. Flavell, *Role Taking and Communication Skills.*

40. Adapted from Selman, R., and Damon, W., "The Necessity (But Insufficiency) of Social Perspective Taking for Conception of Justice at Three Early Levels," in *Moral Development: Current Theory and Research,* ed. D. J. De Palma and J. M. Foley (Hillsdale, N.J.: Lawrence Erlbaum, 1975), pp. 57–75.

41. Iannotti, R. J., The Effects of Role Taking Experiences on Role Taking, Altruism, Empathy, and Aggression (paper presented at the biennial meeting of the Society for Research in Child Development, Denver, April 1975).

42. Rubin and Schneider, "Altruistic Behavior."

43. Krebs and Sturrup, "Behavioral Consistency."

44. Krebs and Sturrup, "Behavioral Consistency."

45. Emler and Rushton, "Cognitive-Developmental Factors." Rushton and Wiener, "Altruism and Cognitive Development."

46. Zahn-Waxler, C., Radke-Yarrow, M., and Brady-Smith, J., "Perspective Taking and Prosocial Behavior," *Developmental Psychology,* 13 (1977):87–88.

47. Krebs, D., "Empathy and Altruism," *Journal of Personality and Social Psychology,* 32 (1975):6, 1134–1146.

48. Piliavin, I. M., Piliavin, J. A., and Rodin, J., "Costs, Diffusion and the Stigmatized Victim," *Journal of Personality and Social Psychology,* 32 (1975):429–438.

49. Eisenberg-Berg, N., and Mussen, P., "Empathy and Moral Development in Adolescence" (manuscript, 1977).

50. Mehrabian, A., and Epstein, N. A., "A Measure of Emotional Empathy," *Journal of Personality,* 40 (1972):523–543.

51. Staub, E., "Use of Role Playing and Induction in Training for Prosocial Behavior," *Child Development,* 42 (1971):805–816.

52. *Ibid.*

53. Iannotti, "Role Taking Experiences."

Chapter 9

1. Hugo, Victor, *Les Miserables*
2. Erickson, E., *Gandhi's Truth* (New York: Norton, 1969).
3. Berkowitz, L., and Conner, W. H., "Success, Failure, and Social Responsibility," *Journal of Personality and Social Psychology,* 4 (1966):664–669. Midlarsky, E., "Aiding Under Stress: The Effects of Competence, Dependency, Visibility, and Fatalism," *Journal of Personality,* 39 (1971):132–149. Midlarsky, E., and Midlarsky, M., "Aiding Under Stress: The Effects of Competence, Status, and Cost to the Aider," *Proceedings of the 78th Annual Convention of the American Psychological Association,* 3 (1970):439–440. Isen, A. M., "Success, Failure, Attention, and Reaction to Others: The Warm Glow of Success," *Journal of Personality and Social Psychology,* 15 (1970):294–301. Isen, A. M., Clark, M., and Schwartz, M. F., "Duration of the Effect of Good Mood on Helping: 'Footprints on the Sands of Time,' " *Journal of Personality and Social Psychology,* 34 (1976):385–393. Rosenhan, D. L., Underwood, B., and Moore, B. S., "Affect Moderates Self-Gratification and Altruism," *Journal of Personality and Social Psychology,* 30 (1974):546–552. Moore, B. S., Underwood, B., and Rosenhan, D. L., "Affect and Altruism," *Developmental Psychology,* 8 (1973):99–104. Isen, A. M., Horn, N., and Rosenhan, D. L., "Effects of Success and Failure on Children's Generosity," *Journal of Personality and Social Psychology,* 27 (1973):239–247.
4. Rosenhan, Underwood, and Moore, "Affect Moderates Self-Gratification and Altruism."
5. Isen, Horn, and Rosenhan, "Success and Failure."
6. Olejnik, A. B., "The Effects of Reward Deservedness on Children's Sharing," *Child Development,* 47 (1976):380–385. Long, G. T., and Lerner, M. J., "Deserving, the 'Personal Contract,' and Altruistic Behavior by Children," *Journal of Personality and Social Psychology,* 29 (1974):551–556. Staub, E., "Children's Sharing Behavior: Success and Failure, the Norm of Deserving and Reciprocity" (paper presented at the biennial meeting of the Society for Research in Child Development, Philadelphia, March 1973).

7. Barnett, M. A., "Effects of Competition and Relative Deservedness of the Other's Fate on Children's Generosity," *Developmental Psychology,* 11 (1975):665–666. McGuire, J. M., and
Thomas, M. H., "Effects of Sex, Competence and Competition
on Sharing Behavior in Children," *Journal of Personality and Social
Psychology,* 32 (1975):490–494.

8. Isen, Clark, and Schwartz, "Effect of Good Mood on Helping."

9. Isen, "Reaction to Others."

10. Aderman, D., "Elation, Depression, and Helping Behavior,"
Journal of Personality and Social Psychology, 24 (1972):91–101.

11. Staub, E., *The Development of Prosocial Behavior in Children* (Mor-
ristown, N.J.: General Learning Press, 1975).

12. Moore, Underwood, and Rosenhan, "Affect and Altruism."
Cialdini, R. B., and Kenrick, D. T., "Altruism as Hedonism: A
Social Development Perspective on the Relationship of Nega-
tive Mood State and Helping," *Journal of Personality and Social
Psychology,* 34 (1976):907–914.

13. Barnett, M. A., and Bryan, J. H., "Effects of Competition with
Outcome Feedback on Children's Helping Behavior," *Development Psychology,* 10 (1974):838–842. Harris, M. B., and Siebel,
C. E., "Affect, Aggression, and Altruism," *Developmental Psychology,* 11 (1975):623–627. McGuire and Thomas, "Sharing
Behavior." Rosenhan, Underwood, and Moore, "Affect Moderates Self-Gratification and Altruism."

14. Isen, Horn, and Rosenhan, "Success and Failure."

15. Aderman, D., and Berkowitz, L., "Observational Set, Empathy,
and Helping," *Journal of Personality and Social Psychology,* 14
(1970):141–148. Steele, C. M., "Name Calling and Compliance," *Journal of Personality and Social Psychology,* 31
(1975):363–369. Apsler, R., "Effects of Embarrassment on Behavior Toward Others," *Journal of Personality and Social Psychology,*
32 (1975):1, 145–153. Freedman, J. L., and Doob, A. N., *De-
viance: The Psychology of Being Different* (New York: Academic
Press, 1968). Filter, T. A., and Gross, A. E., "Effects of Public
and Private Deviancy on Compliance with a Request," *Journal
of Experimental Social Psychology,* 11 (1975):553–559. Kidd,
R. F., and Berkowitz, L., "Effect of Dissonance Arousal on
Helpfulness," *Journal of Personality and Social Psychology,* 33

(1976):613–622. Cialdini, R. B., Darley, B. L., and Vincent, J. E., "Transgression and Altruism: A Case for Hedonism," *Journal of Experimental Social Psychology,* 9 (1973):502–516. Konecni, V. J., "Some Effects of Guilt on Compliance: A Field Replication," *Journal of Personality and Social Psychology,* 23 (1972):30–32. Rawlings, E. K., "Witnessing Harm to Others: A Reassessment of the Role of Guilt in Altruistic Behavior," *Journal of Personality and Social Psychology,* 10 (1968):377–380. McMillen, D. L., Jackson, J. A., and Austin, J. B., "Effects of Positive and Negative Requests on Compliance Following Transgression," *Psychonomic Science,* 24 (1971):59–61. Regan, D. T., Williams, M., and Sparling, S., "Voluntary Expiation of Guilt: A Field Experiment," *Journal of Social Psychology,* 24 (1972):42–45.

16. Cialdini, Darley, and Vincent, "Transgression and Altruism."

17. Cialdini and Kenrick, "Altruism as Hedonism."

18. Fischer, W. F., "Sharing in Preschool Children as á Function of Amount and Type of Reinforcement," *Genetic Psychology Monographs,* 68 (1963):215–245.

19. Azrin, N., and Lindsley, O., "The Reinforcement of Cooperation Between Children," *Journal of Abnormal and Social Psychology,* 2 (1956):100–102. Mithaug, E. D., and Burgess, R. L., "The Effects of Different Reinforcement Contingencies in the Development of Social Cooperation," *Journal of Experimental Child Psychology,* 6 (1968):402–426. Vogler, R. E., Masters, W. M., and Merrill, G. S., "Shaping Cooperative Behavior in Young Children," *Journal of Psychology,* 74 (1970):181–186. Vogler, R. E., Masters, W. M., and Merrill, G. S., "Extinction of Cooperative Behavior as a Function of Acquisition by Shaping or Instruction," *Journal of Genetic Psychology,* 119 (1971):233–240.

20. Azrin and Lindsley, "Cooperation Between Children."

21. Altman, K., "Effects of Cooperative Response Acquisition on Social Behavior During Free Play," *Journal of Experimental Child Psychology,* 12 (1971):387–395.

22. Hartmann, D. P., Gelfand, D. M., Smith, C. L., Paul, S. C., Cromer, C. C., Page, B. C., and Lebenta, D. V., "Factors Affecting the Acquisition and Elimination of Children's Do

nating Behavior," *Journal of Experimental Child Psychology,* 21 (1976):328–338, *336.*

23. Doland, D. J. and Adelberg, K., "The Learning of Sharing Behavior," *Child Development,* 38 (1967):695–700. Gelfand, D. M., Hartmann, D. P., Cromer, C. C., Smith, C. L., and Page, B. C., "The Effects of Instructional Prompts and Praise on Children's Donation Rates," *Child Development,* 46 (1975): 980–983.

24. Doland and Adelberg, "The Learning of Sharing Behavior."

25. Gelfand et al., "Children's Donation Rates."

26. Bandura, A., *Principles of Behavior Modification* (New York: Holt, Rinehart and Winston, 1969), p. 30.

27. Harris, M. B., "Reciprocity and Generosity: Some Determinants of Sharing in Children," *Child Development,* 41 (1970): 313–328. Elliot, R., and Vasta, R., "The Modeling of Sharing: Effects Associated with Vicarious Reinforcement, Symbolization, Age, and Generalization," *Journal of Experimental Child Psychology,* 10 (1970):8–15.

28. Bryan, J. H., "Model, Affect, and Children's Imitative Altruism," *Child Development,* 42 (1971):2061–2065. Midlarsky, E., and Bryan, J. H., "Affect Expressions and Children's Imitative Altruism," *Journal of Experimental Research in Personality,* 6 (1972):195–203. Rushton, J. P., "Generosity in Children: Immediate and Long Term Effects of Modeling, Preaching, and Moral Judgment," *Journal of Personality and Social Psychology,* 31 (1975):3, 459–466. Rushton, J. P., and Owen, D., "Immediate and Delayed Effects of TV Modeling and Preaching on Children's Generosity," *British Journal of Social and Clinical Psychology,* 14 (1975):309–310.

29. Rushton, "Generosity in Children."

30. Bryan, J. H., and Walbek, N. H., "The Impact of Words and Deeds Concerning Altruism Upon Children," *Child Development,* 41 (1970):747–759.

31. Bryan, J. H. and Walbek, N., "Preaching and Practicing Generosity: Children's Action, and Reactions," *Child Development,* 41 (1970):329–353. Rushton and Owen, "Children's Generosity."

32. Rosenhan, D., "Prosocial Behavior of Children," in *The Young Child: Reviews of Research,* Vol. 2, ed. W. W. Hartup (Washington, D.C.: National Association for the Education of Young Children, 1972), pp. 340–359, *354.*

33. Rushton, "Generosity in Children," Anderson, J. A., and Perlman, D., "Effects of an Adult's Preaching and Responsibility for Hypocritical Behavior on Children's Altruism," *Proceedings of the 81st Annual Convention of the American Psychological Association* (1973): 291–292. Liebert, R. M., and Poulos, R. W., "Eliciting the 'Norm of Giving': Effects of Modeling and Presence of Witnesses on Children's Sharing Behavior," *Proceedings of the 79th Annual Convention of the American Psychological Association,* 6 (1971): 345–346. Midlarsky and Bryan, "Children's Imitative Altruism."

34. Rushton, "Generosity in Children."

35. Midlarsky and Bryan, "Children's Imitative Altruism."

36. Rich, M. E., and Grusec, J. E., "Saying and Doing: Effects of Observer Performance," *Journal of Personality and Social Psychology,* 32 (1975):584–593.

37. Berkowitz, L., and Daniels, L., "Responsibility and Dependency," *Journal of Abnormal and Social Psychology,* 66 (1963):429–436. Berkowitz, L., and Daniels, L., "Affecting the Salience of the Social Responsibility Norm: Effects of Past Help on the Response to Dependency Relationships," *Journal of Abnormal and Social Psychology,* 68 (1964):275–281. Harris, M. B., and Meyer, F. W., "Dependency, Threat, and Helping," *Journal of Social Psychology,* 90 (1973):239–242. Lesk, S., and Zippel, B., "Dependency, Threat, and Helping in a Large City," *Journal of Social Psychology,* 95 (1975):185–186. Midlarsky, "Aiding Under Stress." Schaps, E., "Cost, Dependency and Helping," *Journal of Personality and Social Psychology,* 21 (1972):74–78. Schopler, J., and Mathews, M., "The Influence of the Perceived Causal Locus of Partners' Dependence on the Use of Interpersonal Power," *Journal of Personality and Social Psychology,* 2 (1965): 609–612. Wagner, C., and Wheeler, L., "Model, Need and Cost Effects in Helping Behavior," *Journal of Personality and Social Psychology,* 12 (1969):111–116.

38. Liebert, R. M., Fernandez, L. E., and Gill, L., "Effects of a

'Friendless' Model on Imitation and Prosocial Behavior," *Psychonomic Science,* 16 (1969):81–82.

39. Presibie, R. J., and Kanareff, V. T., "Sharing in Children as a Function of the Number of Sharees and Reciprocity," *Journal of Genetic Psychology,* 116 (1970):31–44. Yarrow, M. R., Scott, P., and Waxler, C. Z., "Learning Concern for Others," *Developmental Psychology,* 8 (1973):240–260. Macaulay, J., "Familiarity, Attraction and Charity," *Journal of Social Psychology,* 95 (1975):27–37. Liebhart, E. H., "Empathy and Emergency Helping: The Effects of Personality, Self Concern, and Acquaintance," *Journal of Experimental Social Psychology,* 8 (1972):404–411.

40. Staub, E., and Sherk, L., "Need for Approval, Children's Sharing Behavior and Reciprocity in Sharing," *Child Development,* 41 (1970):243–252.

41. Gottman, J., Gonso, J., and Rasmussen, B., "Social Interaction, Social Competence, and Friendship in Children," *Child Development,* 46 (1975):709–718.

42. Charlesworth, R., and Hartup, W. W., "Positive Social Reinforcement in the Nursery School Peer Group," *Child Development,* 38 (1967):993–1002.

43. Floyd, J., "Effects of Amount of Reward and Friendship Status of Other on the Frequency of Sharing in Children" (Ph.D. dissertation, University of Minnesota, 1964).

44. Staub, Children's Sharing Behavior. Floyd, "Frequency of Sharing in Children."

45. Barnett, "Children's Generosity."

46. Staub, "Children's Sharing Behavior."

47. Staub, E., "A Child in Distress: The Effects of Focusing Responsibility on Children on Their Attempts to Help," *Developmental Psychology,* 2 (1970):152–153.

48. Korte, C., "Group Effects of Help Giving in an Emergency," *Proceedings of the 77th Annual Convention of the American Psychological Association,* 4 (1969):383–384. Latané, B., and Darley, J. M., *The Unresponsive Bystander: Why Doesn't He Help?* (New York: Appleton-Century-Crofts, 1970). Ross, A. S., "Effect of Increased Responsibility on Bystander Intervention: The Pres-

ence of Children," *Journal of Personality and Social Psychology,* 19 (1971):306–310.

49. Staub, E., "A Child in Distress: The Influence of Age and Number of Witnesses on Children's Attempts to Help," *Journal of Personality and Social Psychology,* 14 (1970):130–140.

Chapter 10

1. Arbuthnot, J., "Modification of Moral Judgment Through Role Playing," *Developmental Psychology,* 11 (1975):3, 319–324. Blatt, M., and Kohlberg, L., "Effects of Classroom Moral Discussion Upon Children's Level of Moral Development," in *Recent Research in Moral Development,* ed. L. Kohlberg (New York: Holt, Rinehart and Winston, in preparation). Hickey, J. E., "The Effects of Guided Moral Discussion Upon Youthful Offenders' Level of Moral Judgment," (Ph.D. dissertation, Boston University, 1972) *Dissertation Abstracts International,* 33 (1972):1551A. Holstein, C., "The Relationship of Children's Moral Judgment to That of Their Parents and to Communication Patterns in the Family" (Ph.D. dissertation, University of California, Berkeley, 1969), *Dissertation Abstracts International,* 31 (1970):1888A–1889A. Tracy, J., and Cross, H., "Antecedents of Shift in Moral Judgment," *Journal of Personality and Social Psychology,* 26 (1973):238–244. Turiel, E., "An Experimental Test of the Sequentiality of Developmental States in the Child's Moral Judgments," *Journal of Personality and Social Psychology,* 3 (1966):611–618.

2. Damon, W., "Early Conception of Justice as Related to the Development of Operational Reasoning" (Ph.D. dissertation, University of California, Berkeley, 1974). Ugurel-Semin, R., "Moral Behavior and Moral Judgment of Children," *Journal of Abnormal and Social Psychology,* 47 (1952):463–474. Eisenberg, N. H., "The Development of Prosocial Moral Judgment and Its Correlates" (Ph.D. dissertation, University of California, Berkeley, 1976).

3. Damon, W., *The Social World of the Child* (San Francisco: Jossey-Bass, forthcoming).

4. Erikson, E. H., *Young Man Luther* (New York: Norton, 1958).
    Erikson, E. H., *Gandhi's Truth* (New York: Norton, 1969). Erik-
    son, E. H., *Dimensions of a New Identity* (New York: Norton, 1974).
5. Block, J. H., Haan, N., and Smith, M. B., "Socialization Cor-
    relates of Student Activism," *Journal of Social Issues,* 25 (4)
    (1969):143–177. Haan, N., Smith, M. B., and Block, J. H.,
    "Moral Reasoning of Young Adults: Political-Social Behavior,
    Family Background, and Personality Correlates," *Journal of Per-
    sonality and Social Psychology,* 10 (1968):183–201.
6. Hoffman, M. L., "Developmental Synthesis of Affect and Cog-
    nition and Its Implications for Altruistic Motivation," *Develop-
    mental Psychology,* 11 (1975):607–622.
7. Main, M., "Analysis of a Peculiar Form of Reunion Behavior
    Seen in Some Young Daycare Children," in *Social Development
    in Daycare,* ed. R. A. Webb (Baltimore: The Johns Hopkins
    University Press, 1977).
8. Sullivan, H. S., *Conceptions of Modern Psychiatry* (New York: Nor-
    ton, 1940). Ekstein, R., "Psychoanalysis and Education for the
    Facilitation of Positive Human Qualities," *Journal of Social Issues,*
    28 (1972):71–86.

Index